MW00931301

Grief,
I Didn't
Sign Up
for This

Thank you for your support! Blessings Shalita

*Interviews and
stories from people,
just like you,
navigating through
their grief journey.*

Grapsate, LLC.

Greif, I Didn't Sign Up for This
Copyright © 2023 by Shaleka M. Smith

Request for information should be addressed to
Grapsate, LLC P.O. Box 6443 Evanston, IL 60204

ISBN 978-1-312-51419-5

Any internet address (websites, blogs, etc.) and telephone numbers in this book are offered as a resource. They are not intended in any way to be or imply an endorsement by Shaleka Smith or Grapsate, LLC. Nor does Shaleka Smith or Grapsate, LLC vouch for the content of these sit6es and numbers for he life of this book.

All rights reserved. No part of this publication may be reproduced, stored in a retrieval system, or transmitted in any form or by any means – electronic, mechanical, photocopy, recording, or any other – except for brief quotations in printed reviews, without the prior permission of the author and publisher.

Cover design: Shaleka Smith
Cover photo: Enyd Scott
Interior design: Shaleka Smith

Grief,
I Didn't
Sign Up
for This

*Interviews and
stories from people,
just like you,
navigating through
their grief journey.*

Shaleka Smith

Table of Contents
Grief, I Didn't Sign Up for This

Introduction

In December 2020, I asked God to help me make sense of the recent events in my life. I'd lost the last two males in my immediate family, and I was slowly dying. I was tormented with regrets and guilt to the point where I wouldn't mind going with them. Not an active plan. More like, "Lord, I can't take this pain every day. Help me or take me. Cause I didn't sign up for this." My prayers were the most vulnerable they'd ever been. I was hurt and angry and talking to God with just that tone. Never disrespectful but 100 percent honest.

Welp, He didn't take me. Thank you, God! Once we were able to peek through my emotions, my prayer shifted a little. As my frustrations were sorted out, I began to pray, "Lord, help me find purpose in what I am going through. I want to come out of this season with more than just loss." I'd experienced loss before in life—uncles, brother, father, a best friend, grandmother, and an aunt. All significant to me but with different impacts. However, like most people, the grieving process was about making it look like I was unaffected. Who taught us that?

Not many people will escape life without an encounter with grief. The chance that someone will die before us is high, between family, friends, and just someone we know. Not to mention the things we grief not related to death. We develop relationships with significant impact, and the loss of those relationships crushes us. We are taken into a storm zone. Uncontrolled elements can leave our lives seemingly destroyed. We try to keep ourselves together, but the more we try to be "normal," the more intense the storm gets.

I didn't change my narrative to what made other people comfortable. Ask me how I am doing, and you will get the truth. Call me when I am having a bad moment, and you are going to get these tears. I had no desire to mask my grief. This allowed others to be comfortable sharing their grief stories with me. I began to realize I was not alone. People are always grieving, but we don't talk about it. Who taught us that?

As my grief community developed, God began to show me just how important talking about grief is for the healing process. Wounds don't heal properly if you ignore them and never tend to them. So, I sought a therapist and attended Grief Share, a support group. The more I heard people describing my grief in their stories, I knew that grief had to be talked about. Grief is like a fingerprint, no two people's match, but from far enough away, it looks the same. Hurt.

I want this book to be a relational place. People can see their grief through the writer's story in one way or another. This is not a Self Help Book. This is a Community Book. So we can step out of our grief isolation long enough to see that we aren't alone and be encouraged. This book includes stories from parents, children, siblings, friends, clergy, and clinicians. Odds are, you'll relate to someone.

So, grab your tea or coffee and hear the hearts of people like you. Grievers who never signed up for this.

It's Gonna Hurt

Anonymous

I wish someone had told me about the pain that comes from someone you love dying.

I would have braced myself.

Braced me for the feeling that my world was ending.

Braced me for the anger I felt.

Braced me for the confusion I felt.

Braced me from being so overwhelmed with emotions that I went numb.

Everyone who has experienced grief knows it's gonna hurt. So why does no one ever tell you how much? Why is the hurt from loss never the topic of conversation? There are so many layers of pain. First, the pain from knowing that you will never see a person again, never hold their hand, and never share any memories with them. It's overwhelming, and a part of you dies with them. You don't just grieve the physical person; you grieve the spiritual connection, and that's the worst part.

When I received the news that my great grandma had passed away, I had no reaction. I lived with her at the time and was around her quite often. Any average person would be sad or even crying. Not me. It sounds terrible, but I just carried on with my life. Or at least that's how it seemed to everyone around me. In the beginning, it wasn't about me. I had to be strong for everyone around me. My family was breaking down, and I felt I had to be strong. We couldn't all be broken down. When things finally settled down with them, it was my turn. By then, I was overloaded with different emotions, and my body began to shut down. I used numbness as a coping mechanism. I could not allow myself to cry because I would cry too hard. I would be viewed as vulnerable. I would be forced to feel the actual feelings my body was working so hard to suppress. I couldn't look at pictures or hear any conversations with her name comfortably. I just wanted to erase it all from my memory because that was easier.

Grief is hard. There is no right or wrong way to grieve. However, taking care of yourself and the people experiencing grief with you is imperative. I found strength in talking to people about what I was experiencing. I saw a counselor and joined a grief support group. Those two things helped me process the reality of what was going on. I began to realize that just because I physically don't have my great grandma with me anymore does not mean she is no longer around. Her spirit is still in my heart and my memories. I still talk to her. She can't respond audibly, but things happen to make me feel her presence. Sometimes I think of her, remember her saying something, and hear her voice. She is with me. We are connected. People should always cherish the people that they have because you never know when they will be gone. I cherish every moment, but I still wish I had more. I will never be over losing my great grandma. I have adapted to not having her, but it doesn't mean I am over it. I don't actively cry all the time, but I'm okay.

Get Up

Anonymous

"If you wouldn't have left, I wouldn't have left."

As much as I knew that was true, it wouldn't have changed my decision to leave. Divorce isn't how I wanted my marriage to end. I loved my husband, and he loved me. I never questioned that. However, there are three things I have no tolerance for; physical abuse, emotional abuse, and infidelity.
Unfortunately, my husband decided to go with the latter.

We got married when we were just 19 years old. We were high school sweethearts. I was so happy to be his wife. Taking care of him and our child gave me so much joy. I enjoyed every part of our lives. We didn't have much, but it was ours. Our home, our family, our love. I loved being a wife and mother. It looked good on me. It looked good on us. I honestly never imagined him committing adultery. In my mind, it wasn't possible. It wasn't an option.

A year into our marriage, I learned how much of an option it was. My husband, who was my knight in shining armor, became a villain in our fairy tale. His evil actions destroyed what I wanted to be a perfect marriage. I knew there was a shift when he went from hanging out with his friends' wearing jeans and gym shoes to giving extra attention to his appearance. He started dressing nice, button-up shirts, sweaters, slacks, and nice shoes. He almost gave himself away. As time went on, I didn't know what was happening, but I quickly became a private investigator. I quickly found something that would break me into a million pieces.

Sonogram Images.

My husband was going to have a baby with another woman.

I had never felt so betrayed. All I could hear was
his *mothers* voice, "if you marry him, you will be marrying
his father." To most people, that would be a positive
statement. Not for us. His father had cheated on his mother.
What a family trait. For a brief moment, I wondered if he
could help it. That thought faded when I felt my heart
physically breaking in my chest. I never knew pain like it.
How could he cheat on ME? I was a good loving wife. At that
moment, I learned a life lesson I wish I'd been taught earlier.
Sometimes love is not enough. No. Love is not enough.

I knew my husband loved me. Anyone that was ever around
us knew that the love we had was authentic. I never felt
unloved. I felt betrayed. My husband had developed a
relationship with a woman he couldn't let go of. Shortly after I
learned about the pregnancy, the woman decided to have an
abortion. My husband was devastated. He knew he couldn't
keep the baby and his marriage. He chose his marriage. The
affair ended. He was trying. Yet over time, they found their
way back to one another.

That was hard to process. The emotions were endless. I slowly
slide into depression. The thing I loved doing the most, taking
care of my family. Stopped. I no longer had joy in the very
things that made me happy. Taking care of my husband.
Taking care of my son. Being domestic. Taking care of
everyone and everything was no longer at the top of my
priority list. Truth be told, not only were those things not
priorities, they weren't options. My only options at this point
were to drink alcohol and isolate myself. *Isolate me* from my
husband, my siblings, and my child. I barely went to work. It
was a very dark time in my life. I was grieving.

I don't know that I knew that it was grief at that moment. All I knew was that my life was shaken up like a snow globe. My identity as a wife, soul mate, and life partner had died. I had been so consumed with building my family that I wasn't aware of what other things defined me. I appreciate my younger siblings, who stepped up and cared for my son. But I also understand that his preschool self didn't recognize something was wrong. All he knew was that he had what he needed.

Me drowning my emotions with alcohol, and seclusion went on for about a year. Then, one Sunday, I was listening to a local radio station that played gospel music. A song came on by Helen Baylor, "Can you Reach My Friend." I cried and began to do something that wasn't a part of my daily routine. I prayed. I prayed that God would help my husband see what he was doing to our family. Prayed that God would change his heart. Prayed that God would reach him in a way that I couldn't. I asked a lot of God that day on behalf of my husband. The more I prayed, the more I realized my husband wasn't who needed to be reached. It was me. I was the friend that needed to know that God loved them, and that God was the only one who could help me through this. I didn't get to where I was overnight, so it wouldn't bounce back quickly. However, that day, I decided to GET UP.

I decided to function with a broken heart and a new reality. I embraced that the forever I thought I had was simply just a chapter in my book of life. I got up and began to put my life back together. I reclaimed my domestic responsibilities. I became present again for my son. I extended an olive branch to my husband. I stayed with him. I presented the option for counseling. I wanted it to be clear that I was willing to do whatever it took to keep what we had. What we built. I didn't want to leave any rock unturned if we had to walk away from one another.

Getting up required me to face the reality that things don't always turn out as you want them to. After only five years of marriage, I decided that the situation wasn't one I was okay with and didn't deserve. The grieving continued. Grief went beyond the failed marriage. I went from living in our tiny house to living in an apartment. I went from having a two-income home to now being a single mother and struggling financially. Before this chapter in my life, I never walked into my house and flipped the lights to confirm that our electricity was not disconnected. Before this chapter in my life, I always went with a meal. There were days that my son ate, but I didn't. Before this chapter, I had a co-parent. I had to deal with the struggle of my son living between the two households. Requiring regular reprogramming. I had to navigate the frustration I felt when my son would go visit his father and the mistress-turned-wife. There were no boundaries or financial limitations because that was a two-income home. Grief presented itself when my son grew older and realized that his father was less than perfect.

Grief has a negative reputation no matter what you are grieving. Unfortunately, no one ever shares what you can gain from a grief experience. One of the major positive things that comes out of grief is wisdom. Very often, wisdom should and could be shared with others. It has been many years since my marriage ended. I struggled with the fact that I didn't have positive examples of marriage or anyone to share their wisdom with me. I thank God that I am on the other side of it now. If I had a daughter, I would share the truth with her about relationships and marriage in hopes that hers never ended like mine. However, if it did, she would be better equipped to handle the grief that comes with that loss. So, the advice I would give is to make sure, at some point, you GET UP.

Why No One Asked

As told by Cheryl Johnson

As I sit back and think about my best friend, so many feelings come back to me, the ones I swept under the rug. She was my favorite person. She was fun to be around. Way more than my mother! My grandmother, Esther, was the best. I spent as much time with her as I could. It usually worked in my favor since she was my grandmother and loved having me around. I wasn't the only grandchild, but many of my memories were only her and me. Our relationship was so special. When she died, I was lost without her. Who would I have?

My maternal grandmother was such a kind and gentle person. I don't know if that is in the grandmother's job description, but she was overqualified in that area. I was always comfortable around her. I wasn't restricted there, like at my mother's house. My mother wasn't as open to talking about things as Grandma Esther. That's challenging, considering most children have more questions than a standardized test. However, my grandmother welcomed queries and conversations. She had so much wisdom. I don't think there was ever a time I asked a question, and she didn't have an answer. Which always had me coming back for more answers. Not only did she answer all my questions, but she also always told me stories from when she was younger. "I remember when" was a phrase I heard often. I enjoyed hearing her take trips down memory lane.

Not only my fountain of wisdom, but she was also my culinary instructor. Anytime she was in the kitchen, I was right there with her. She taught me to cook so many things. She was never in a rush when she was teaching me something. She always took her time and showed me exactly what to do. One day at work, I thought of her and this one dish she would make and went home and duplicated it. Once I mastered it, I made it for my children often. I called it "The Concoction." It includes ground beef sauteed with onions, tomatoes, garlic, and spaghetti. The next step was to put it in the oven. She served it with green beans. I added a twist and replaced the spaghetti with tri-colored pasta. Now that my youngest daughter lives independently, she has also tried it.

Grandma Esther passed down more generational blessings than cooking. I feel like she was intentional about ensuring positive examples at her house. She showed me how to be generous and thoughtful. My mom was an only child and not accustomed to sharing her mother. Perhaps she was jealous of the relationship between Grandma Esther and me. I am not sure what their relationship was when my mother was a child, but I remember that she wasn't herself after my grandmother had brain surgery. I remember my mother not being very kind to my grandmother. It was odd for me and often had me frustrated with my mom. I remember hearing her cry at my grandmother's funeral and thinking, "Oh, now you want to cry?"

I know it sounds harsh, but I have my reasons.

My grandmother worked for a family doing light housework. After she did not show up to work one day, the lady called my mom and expressed concern. My mother seemed bothered that she had to go to my grandmother's. I was at home, and she asked me to go with her. In the days leading up to this, I had this feeling I needed to see my grandmother. I was 17 and didn't understand the importance of listening to your first thoughts. I don't remember what I was thinking on our way to my grandmother's house that day, but I didn't expect what we walked into.

My grandmother was dead. She was face down on the floor between her living room and kitchen doorway. If I close my eyes, I can still see her. It was indeed one of the hardest things I've ever dealt with. We don't know how long she had been there, but her body was cold and stiff. I don't know if I had ever imagined my grandmother dying. I assumed she would always be around. But I was standing there looking at the body of the woman I knew truly loved me. My mother called 911, but there was nothing for paramedics to do. There was no bringing her back. I wasn't ready for that.

Taking the time to write down my feelings, I've had the opportunity to look at the situation from a different perspective. I am older and have had several family members die since my grandmother. I would have loved to have my grandmother around a while longer. I remember having my first child and wishing she could be there. Showing my daughter, the same love she showed me. Her love and our time together prepared me to live without her. She taught me so much and planted so many seeds. None were visible at 17 years old, but as the years have gone on, I've seen all that she put in me. The Bible talks about one planting, one watering, and God getting the increase. She was my planter, and life has been my water.

As a late teen and young adult, I can't say I knew how to grieve. I'd never lost anyone who impacted my life as my grandmother did. Plenty of my family members had. No one ever made sure that I knew how to process death. I don't even think anyone asked me how I felt about what was happening. That was problematic. Grieving was lonely for me. I became more shut off than anything. Grief and life's challenges developed weeds that kept those seeds my grandmother planted from growing. I started to take on the negative characteristics of my mother instead of those positive ones my grandmother instilled in me. My walk with God is what helped to clear out the weeds—learning to pray for myself and not to the saints as my Catholic faith had taught me. It was life changing. I began praying to God to break things off of me. I promised I would never be what I saw growing up. I want to be loving, kind, and caring like my grandmother Esther. God has and is still changing me. Now I see myself enjoying life the way my grandmother did.

My Daddy

Andrea Corley-Gardner

On June 11, 1998, my heart broke into a million pieces.

My dad died.

At first, I felt numb, but then a sense of rage, sorrow, and confusion overcame me. I'll never forget getting into my car and driving with no destination. I turned on the radio, and "Be Encouraged" by William Beckton came on. Tears flowed down my face, listening to the words trying to make sense of it. How was I supposed to be encouraged? My daddy was gone—one of the most influential people in my world. I did not know if this was meant for me or if I was supposed to be encouraging someone else. I didn't have it in me to encourage anyone. I didn't even have it in me to get out of the car when I finally made it home. I eventually wandered into the house. My whole family was there.

I was looking at my mom, wondering if she was feeling what I was feeling. There was no emotion on her face. My mother, his wife, didn't cry. She didn't seem worried. Nothing. What is happening? My dad is gone forever. No hugs, no kisses, no phone calls. No snuggling under him. No more of him fussing at me about my car. Nothing. I was not able to hear him call me Carmencita anymore. All the things I would miss began to flood my thoughts. I began feeling angry. Why did God take my dad from me? I started shutting down again. Feeling numb. I didn't know what to do. Is this normal? God, why would you do this to us? The days up until the funeral just seemed to pass by.

We had two funerals for my dad—one in Chicago and another in Mississippi, where he would be buried. My paternal grandmother lived in Mississippi, and she did not travel. The first funeral seemed like a dress rehearsal. I remember just being there. Nothing moved me. Nothing was memorable. Perhaps it was because it wasn't the final moments. I would see him again in Mississippi. I had one more time.

It was June 22, 1998, and the final day. Father's Day. This was the moment I wasn't ready for. I was watching everyone move around getting dressed. I just sat looking. Wondering why my grandma wasn't getting dressed. As Dad's siblings were in the room talking to her, I heard her yell, "I will not participate in seeing my son buried." I thought she was not going to say goodbye to her son. Who does that? I can't imagine losing one of my boys. But I couldn't understand why she wouldn't want to go. I went into the room and sat next to her. I can still remember the look on her face and the hurt in her voice. I asked her, "Grandma, why are you not going to the funeral?" She replied, "Baby, I don't want to see my son laying lifeless in no box." Maybe I didn't either, but I needed closure. I needed to say goodbye to my daddy. I needed to tell him how much I loved him. Hug him one more time.

While everyone was dressed to the T, I put on my daddy's favorite dress to see me in and this bright red lipstick that he talked about when he saw me. The funeral was packed. People were standing outside waiting to pay their respects. At that moment, I realized my dad was truly loved. As the service was ending, it was time for the final viewing. As I walked up to my dad's casket, stood there. I couldn't move. I just wanted him to get up and say, "SURPRISE, Carmencita." He didn't; he couldn't. I remember saying I love you and kissing him. Placing a Father's Day shirt I had purchased in the casket. Then it happened. I screamed at the top of my lungs, "Daddy, don't leave me!" Crying profusely, I felt my mom grab me. I didn't know how to feel. I kept screaming, "Daddy, don't leave me!" I don't remember how I made it to the burial. I just remember my uncles folding the American flag that was on his casket and giving it to my mom. I remember seeing the coffin lowered and the cemetery workers throwing dirt in the grave.

Back at the repast, I just sat. I didn't eat, didn't talk to anyone. I just wanted to be left alone. A piece of me was missing; I was incomplete. I didn't even want to be bothered with my own children. The time had come for us to leave and return to Chicago. My aunt thought it was a good idea for me to leave the boys so I could have some "grieving time," whatever that meant. Did she really expect me to grieve my father in a few summer months? I don't think I started grieving at that point, but I had changed. I didn't care about anything. I started drinking and smoking weed and hanging out all night, going to work when I felt like it. I was being very promiscuous. I had no care in the world. I was reckless. Summer was over, and I had to go to Mississippi to pick my boys up. My maternal nature was there; I was a bad mom. I left my kids at my mom's house to party and lived my life.

One day my mom sat me down and confronted me about my behavior. She told me that she didn't like the person I had become. If I were to be honest, I didn't either, but what else was I to do with this pain. She told me I had two beautiful boys that needed me. I was self-destructing, and she refused to lose another person. She said we would get through this together. I asked her, "How? Why did God take Daddy away from us? Aren't you mad at him? "My mom replied, "Andrea, God did not take your father from us. Yes, we can't physically see him, but he still lives. He lives within us. In our thoughts. In our hearts. All the memories we have with him still live on. Through us." I didn't understand what she was saying. She told me when she gets lonely or feels the need to talk to him, she just talks, and I should do the same. She explained to me the circle of life, and because my dad had given his life back to Christ, his spirit still lives. I didn't want to hear any God talk at that moment. She suggested that I start reading my

Bible. I really didn't want to hear that. It wasn't until I had come home high and drunk and my oldest son said to me, "Ma, I don't want you to die," that I knew I needed to change my actions. I had to do this for my kids, but I still felt incomplete.

I didn't know how to begin the healing process. During the day, I would just go through the motions. Work, school, home to be with my boys. At night I would cry myself to sleep. Then one night, I dreamed about my dad. He reassured me that he would always be with me. That he never left me. He told me he wanted me to finish school. Get my life back in order. He said I will always be his "Carmencita." That morning when I woke up, I felt different. I felt almost normal. That morning my healing process began. Although I still think I am not truly healed from my dad's death, I can say I'm in a better place. There are days I miss him tremendously. Times when I know if he were here physically, I wouldn't need people to do things for me. I still get emotional whenever I hear "Be Encouraged" on the radio. I know now that my dad does live within me, and while the flesh is absent, his spirit is much alive.

I'm Better

As told by Amber Johnson

I was his shadow. I followed him everywhere. If he left the house and I was able to go, I did. I enjoyed being around him. It was our time. Even just a store run was our store run. Most girls adore their fathers. I was no different. He was one of my favorite people in the world, especially when I was a child. He always made me feel important to him. He was always just as happy to see me as I was to see him. He made me laugh. He talked to me like I was his friend. I was his little buddy, and he was mine.

Of the 16 years I had with my dad, most were filled with positive memories. He was a hardworking man. He had his struggles, but none of that changed how I felt about him. When he and my mother started having their marital problems, there was a shift. The time he and I spent together did not decrease; our conversations changed. He went from talking to me like his daughter to talking to me like one of his friends or brothers. I heard things that no child should hear about their parents' relationship. There were no boundaries. The more he confided in me, the more uncomfortable I was. There was a tug-of-war over whose side to be on, my mother's or my father's. I wish adults understood that the problems they have are never just between them. Children are highly affected by toxic environments. Behavior changes, and very often, academic performance declines. That was my case. My teachers noticed. My parents did not. Finally, my teachers were concerned enough to bring things to my parents' attention. They did their best, but not much changed.

I have never been good at appropriately managing my emotions or expressing my feelings. My environment taught me what not to do but never what to do. I did not know how to tell my parents that their issues were destroying me. I internalized everything. Their problems were now mine. I did not have the power to help them or myself. To avoid being at home, I started getting involved in extra-curricular activities. My plan worked, kind of. I was never home, but my father was my transportation most of the time. Those rides were not very long, so there wasn't much venting to be heard. Yet enough to still be affected. By the time I was in high school, I had developed an "avoid home" plan that worked for me.

My plan did not minimize the depression that was developing. I was busy, but when I had a moment to sit with my thoughts, my brain went to a dark place. I would self-harm to cope. I did not know any other way to release my emotions. I had spent several years wishing I could fix things yet realizing that I couldn't. But dads? Aren't they supposed to be fixers? Why wasn't my dad making things better? I do not know if stuff with my parents could have been better. Their hate for one another grew. I wondered why they stayed together. Why wouldn't my dad just move out if things were that bad? Why would anyone stay somewhere where no one was happy? Maybe if he had removed himself from the situation, it would have alleviated stress for my parents, my sister, and me. If I could have a conversation with my dad today, I would want to know, "What made you stay?"

I have wondered if my dad ever considered leaving to bring peace to our household. Did he know what the chronic disruption in our environment would do to us, to me? Perhaps he never viewed the constant arguing as a problem because he was raised in a similar environment. What you see is what you know. What you know guides your behavior. I have so many questions and thoughts. There are a lot of things I was not old enough to talk with him about, or even had the courage to say. Before the time came for me to have a voice, he died.

My dad picked me up from school and activities often, so the day that he did not show up was odd. His tardiness had my mom, sister, and me in a frenzy. The two of them were concerned with who he could be with. My concern was that he would never leave me stranded. Something must have been wrong. My sister came to get me in his absence. While driving, my sister was talking to my mom on the phone about who my dad could be with. Something in me did not think that was the case.

Daddy would not forget me.

We turned a corner, and there was his car. Not parked but out of the way of traffic. Something was not right. Why would he be pulled over here? Why is he parked like that? The conversation I was having with myself was louder than the phone conversation between my mom and sister. We seemed to all arrive at his car at the same time. We exited our cars and walked toward his from opposite directions. My sister and I approached from the front of the car and my mother from the back. Then I heard it. A high-pitched scream. It was not familiar to me. It was my mom. I followed her gaze into my dad's car. The anger that had been brewing quickly turned to shock.

His face. I will never forget his face. He looked like a flash went off, and he was stuck in a trance. Stiff. Like he was frozen at that moment. His car was pulled over to the curb like he felt that something was not right and needed to get out of the way. I thank God that he did not crash. I do not remember how the EMTs were called, but they came. He was removed from the car and taken to the hospital. He had gone into cardiac arrest, and he couldn't be revived.

I miss my dad. He was my dad. No one can change that relationship. However, I acknowledge that I was in a dark place in my adolescence, and he contributed to that. Was it intentional? Of course not. Yet he did not make much effort for improvements if he even noticed. So, I have mixed feelings about wanting him back. I would love for him to see all that I've accomplished. However, I do not think I would have been able to do any of it if he were still alive. It is hard to admit that because we never want to speak ill of the dead. Sometimes the truth is that we love people dearly because of who they are to us, but if it were not for those connections, we wouldn't choose them.

He's Family

As told by Aixa Lopez

When did he transition from being my abuser to family?

There was never a transition. He was always both. More
family than abuser since I really did not know I had been
abused. Being molested by him at the age of four did not
translate in my mind as abuse. It did not even translate into
being wrong. I could say it was standard. He was not the only
person who touched me. There were several family members,
both men and women, that violated my tiny body. It was what
people did. I did not know this was inappropriate behavior
until I was in fifth grade when the good old D.A.R.E. program
came to our school and explained two things: drugs and
inappropriate touching. After hearing all the presenter had to
say, I felt like I had done something wrong.

I remember going home and sitting on the front steps. That is
a lot of information for a fifth grader to attempt to process. All
this time, it was wrong. All this time, I was being hurt. Maybe
he didn't know it was wrong. He was only five years older
than me. He told me it was a secret, so, yeah, he must have
known it was terrible. But why would someone that's
supposed to love me because we're family hurt me? Why
would any of them hurt me? It must have been written all over
my face. A neighbor saw me and with a simple, "What's
wrong?" the words poured out like a waterfall.

Like a good neighbor, they went to my parents, which hadn't
really seemed like an option to me. Perhaps it was because I
also wondered why my parents did not do a better job of
protecting me. Don't get me wrong, I have the best parents,
but as a child, I was often left with other people. People they
thought I was safe with because they were family. Children
should always be safe around family. That was not my case.

Family is where I was violated. I didn't share about the other abusers with the neighbor. The focus was on my cousin. Yet, at that moment, he wasn't family. He was my abuser. He wasn't the only person in my family who had touched me inappropriately. But, he was the first abuser. As I got older, my frustration was directed at him.

My father was furious and was looking for the nephew who had abused his daughter. At that point, my abuser fled the state to New York. I do not remember exactly when he returned. I just know that when he did, I was older, and we were back to being family. Like in most families, the abuse was not public information. So, you sweep the abuser part under the rug at family events. It is not that he was forgiven. I wasn't actively mad. Self-destructing, yes, but not actively mad at him or any of them. I was angry at the world. Anyone could get the wrath of Aixa; many people did. I spent my teenage years and early twenties taking my pain out on everyone. Angry. Aggressive. Violent. My misplaced anger gave me a reputation—one I have worked hard to escape.

I remember when I decided to try God. I wanted to really understand what being a believer meant. Very often, people create unrealistic expectations of what being a Christian is— not based on Biblical truth but on their own biases. I was not interested in fulfilling anyone's expectations of me. Instead, I needed to learn what it meant to forgive. Not the artificial forgiveness people offer one another with their lips, but not their hearts. I needed my heart to be right. I'd walked around for way too long with a hardened heart and feared what would happen if I did not get it together. This effort could not have happened at a more perfect time.

I was at work and received a direct internal message from my sister, who also worked for the company. As usual, she told me to come to her desk. What I did not know was that she'd already contacted our manager to inform them that we needed to leave due to a death in our family. When I got to her desk, she told me that my abuser was found unresponsive at my aunt's house.

I was devastated. At that moment, he was family. He wasn't this horrible person; he wasn't my abuser. It was my *cousin* who wasn't well. I remember traveling to the hospital. There were a lot of moving parts. His best friend was in the car with us. Neither my sister nor I disclosed much information. Only that we needed to get to the hospital. I think for me, there was a hope that he wasn't dead. As we walked down the hall and got closer to the room, his sister yelled down the hall that he was dead.

At that moment, two people died, my abuser and my cousin. I remember screaming, "I forgive him, I forgive him. I am sorry. I don't hold it anymore." At that moment, my plea was in desperation for him to come back. It was a feeling that everything that I was holding was the cause of his death and not the drugs. I felt like my anger killed him. Maybe my forgiveness could bring him back, and I wouldn't have to see my family hurt. Though I said these things in a moment of desperation, I did forgive him.

I forgave him because I now had a Biblical understanding of forgiveness. The same grace extended to me by God for all the things I've done wrong in life is the same grace that God expected me to lend to others. Even if they didn't apologize, forgive them. Even if they aren't sorry, forgive them. Even if you never get to confront them about their actions, forgive them. Forgive them because it heals you. Forgive them because it keeps you in covenant with God. Forgive them because God forgave you.

The forgiveness allowed me to experience the moment of mourning with my family that anger wouldn't have allowed. We all were mourning the loss of the same person but in different relationships. His mother lost a child. His daughter lost a father. His sister lost a brother. I lost my cousin. I've learned that people shouldn't be defined by mistakes they've made in their lifetime. They should be defined by who they are today. Today he is my cousin that took me on my first motorcycle ride. He is the person who looked after my brother when he was struggling. He is the father of one amazing little girl that he didn't get to see grow up. Today he is my cousin.

My Friend

As told by DeAnna Gibson

Forty-year-olds do not die.

Not in my life. Not my circle. She was not sickly. She just got sick. She was not dying. She just died. She was not ready. She just went. Dionesha was the oldest of the five of us. She carried being the oldest with honor like most big sisters do. She loved us dearly and wanted the best for us. She was always encouraging us and gently pushing us to be all that God called us to be. Great women, great wives, great mothers, great stewards over all that we are responsible for. Especially ourselves. She was our very own cheerleader. I miss that about her. I think she would be so happy for the growth we've all experienced since she's been gone.

I never expected our relationship to blossom the way it did. In 2013, she and her family came to a church service. I was the last of our friends to meet her. My life increased when she became part of it. If she loved you, you knew it. She was so thoughtful. She would buy us "just because" gifts and save them for us. Birthdays were a holiday. I have so many cards and handwritten notes to go back and read when I want to hear her voice. I've kept our text messages so that I can go back and read them. When someone dies, a cap is placed on the memories you can create with them. The memories we have are all we will ever have. She will not be around for so many memorable moments. Especially for her daughter. No more first days of school. No graduations. No wedding. No grandchildren. We will all have moments where we will wish she were here. There will not be a moment in her daughter's life when she won't need her mother. That bothers me. I am in my thirties and couldn't imagine life without my mother.

There is a constant conflict for me when it comes to the death of my friend. Not only that she was relatively young, but she wasn't ill. Not deathly ill. We all just knew she would bounce back. There was nothing in me that thought my friend would die. Not this young. I only consider death for specific groups. I know that death has no limits. I get that; however, I don't understand it. I don't know that anyone will ever have an answer for me. I often pray about it. I have a desperate need for comfort and understanding. Two things that only God can provide. People turn away from God while grieving. I can't. He is my lifeline because sometimes it hurts just that bad where I need Him to help me through that moment. I experience so many different emotions. I, like many other people, prayed for healing for Dee. I prayed, and I believed. But she died. I trust God, but I don't understand why my friend is gone.

I have a tough time wrapping my head around my best friend dying. Even now, three years later, I still cannot believe that Dee is gone. Not like she went on a trip and will be gone for a while. More like she moved away to a faraway land, and we will never be able to talk again. We will never text again. We will never laugh together again. She will never join us for another girl's trip. We will never celebrate our birthdays together. She will never meet my children. We will not be old ladies together that will tell people we've been friends for 40 or 50 years. Death is the only time you can use "never" and know that it is 100 percent never.

I can relate to a comment made at her funeral about people that could have been taken besides her. Death is a part of life, yet I feel like Dee had so much more life to live. Her gifts and talents hadn't reached their peak. She just started working on her branding. She'd started a blog and was looking forward to doing so much. I was looking forward to seeing her reach all her goals. The way she glowed when she spoke about her endeavors encourages me even now. But she didn't get to see them all through. Her death has been a reality check for me. I don't have forever. I pray that I will live a long life, but it won't be forever. Knowing that I don't have all the time in the world pushes me to put more effort into reaching my goals, which is what my friend would want for me. For all of us, really. The four of us have had so much growth since her death, both spiritually and naturally. Though Dee pushed us to have natural growth, she also encouraged spiritual growth. It's beautiful to have friends that can relate on multiple levels. I appreciate her for that.

Dee's death has been the hardest to process, but I know I am not alone. My sister Amanda, Dee's sister Jos, Tina, and I can lean on each other. We grieve together yet so differently. Though we are all friends, our relationships with her were so different. Grief changed life for all of us. It's been challenging to all be together and know our star is missing a point. We spent a lot of time now learning how to function without her. It was uncomfortable in a way. In all honesty, this awkward space has drawn us closer together. We latched on to one another a little tighter. It's now a reality of just how short life is.

Earlier I said she wasn't ready. She just went. Dee thought she would be coming back home. We went to her house after she died. It felt as if she was still there. Her house was always so well put together. Everything had its place. It was just who she was. She was a very orderly person, but there were dishes in the sink. As if to say she'd be back to wash them and put them up. If Dee knew we had to go in her house while she wasn't there, it would have been in tip-top shape. She didn't think she would leave and never come back. I can remember her saying if something happens to one of us, she's right there. She thought this would pass. It didn't, and now I have to live with this hurt in my heart until we meet again. I hope she knows I miss her just as much as I love her.

Bounce

Karena Leonard

July 27, 2021, is a day I will never forget. It was the day I was introduced to grief.

It started at 2:10pm when I received a phone call from my mom while I was headed to work.

"She is gone."

The emotion in her voice was something I'd never heard. Her voice trembled. My mom was crying. That sound was new to me. So were her words. I knew exactly who "she" was. Someone I've known all my life. A woman I've loved and admired. The matriarch of our family. My grandma died. I screamed and cried alone in my car. The wind was knocked out of me. I felt like I needed to do something but didn't know what to do. The news paralyzed me. I sat for what seemed like hours. Then I remembered I had to notify my job of my absence, and I did. I returned home still with no apparent thought of what to do. I paced the floor. Those words kept playing in my head.

She is gone.

She is gone.

She is gone.

I made two phone calls; one was to my best friend. Within minutes she was at my house, and we were headed to my grandma's house. The ride was hazy. Text messages and phone calls flooded my phone. I couldn't tell you who called or texted. My focus was strictly on getting to my grandma.

Though we had to get to the other side of town, the ride went fast.

I walked into the house. People were there, but none of them were relevant at the moment. I needed to see her. I needed to see it for myself. She was lying in the hospital bed she'd been in since coming home. When the doctors told us there was nothing else they could do. Her body was there, lifeless. The moment my eyes fell on her body, my heart hurt. Tears ran down my face.

She is gone.

I never knew grief before that day. We've become better acquainted as time has passed. Following the funeral, this obese uninvited being named grief sat on me. Every time I thought about my grandma, grief would bounce, putting even more weight on me. No matter what I tried, I couldn't get from under it. My world has become dark. I function because I have no choice, but I don't know life without my grandmother. I am the oldest grandchild. I've had her around all my life. What am I supposed to do without her? I need her here. I want her here.

I want to dial her number and hear her voice, excited to hear from me. BOUNCE.

I want to hear her say, "Hey Poo Poo." BOUNCE.

Did God need my grandma more than I did? BOUNCE.

Why did she have to get cancer? BOUNCE.

BOUNCE... BOUNCE... BOUNCE...

For months now, if I hear a song or someone says a phrase reminding me of her, the reality of her not being here overwhelms me. I've always been a loner with just a few friends. I've never had the desire to be around a lot of people. Nothing has changed. If anything, it has gotten worse. I've realized that there is a level of sensitivity that doesn't exist in some people. My wounds are fresh. I am fragile. Now more than any time, I cannot be mishandled. Though I usually can take anything like a champ, I've had no fight. Grief has taken so much out of me.

Having people around that are empathic helps when dealing with the avalanche of emotions that grief brings. The right person can bring you comfort and support at the right moment. The wrong person can do the complete opposite. Most of the time, I have support but not from the person I thought I'd get it. Not from who I've "needed" it. Introducing me to a different type of grief at the same time. I quickly learned that grief doesn't only come when someone dies. Grief comes when anything is lost. Even a relationship.

Before my grandmother died, I wasn't in the perfect relationship. We've been together on and off for over twenty years. People say that when someone shows you who they are, believe them. I believed, but I thought it would be different in the days surrounding my grandmother's death. I assumed. There was no sensitivity to what I was going through. Just imagine and act accordingly, even if you've not experienced a close loss. I learned a new life lesson just hours after my grandmother's funeral. You can grieve someone that is still alive. BOUNCE.

At the height of a confrontation, I lost the last ounce of hope that this person could ever be who I wanted, needed, and deserved for them to be. So now I'd experience two significant losses. My grandmother and my partner. I never felt so abandoned. The people I needed the most during this time were not available. In an unfamiliar place, it helps to have familiar people. I had neither. BOUNCE.

It was evident in this foreign place that God was and is all I have. No grandma. No partner. Just me and God. I've begun talking to Him more. There is nothing that I hide from Him because my grief doesn't leave any space for harbored feelings. God knows my thoughts, my hurt, my sorrow. He created me. So, He also knows how to maintain me. So, I've depended on His compassion, consistency, and fatherly love. The more the relationship develops, the more the void of not having those two people in my life is filled with the presence of God. Some people don't understand what that means. When I need to talk to my grandmother, I speak to God. When I need the support of a partner, I depend on God. When I need my old normal, I remember that God will walk with me in my new normal.

The more I depend on God, the more weight grief loses. The more I am honest with God about my hurt, disappointment, and regrets, the less intense my emotions are. The more I am vulnerable with Him, who knew I would be in this situation, the lighter the bounce is. I trust that one day, my obese grief will wear a size 2, and when the bounce happens, it won't weigh me down. I don't know how long it will take for the impact of the grief to not affect me so severely. However, as I seek God for comfort, I will slowly heal. But to have double loss means I need double God.

Guilt

As told by Milton Butler

My mother was my superhero! The things she was able to make happen for us growing up were jaw-dropping. A single mother of four, she made it look effortless at times. As an adult, I can recognize times when we struggled. However, experiencing it as a child, I felt like things were decent. From time to time, we'd find that our gas or electricity was disconnected. Yet by the end of the day, things were back to normal. I was never concerned about those things because I always knew she would handle it. She was never down long.

It took me a long time to process my mother's death. I can't really say that it's a completed task, but I am much better than I was before. From the moment she was placed in that ambulance, I dealt with an overwhelming amount of guilt. It wasn't my fault, but it took me a long time to even be able to say that. Life is full of regrets, no matter the circumstances. But to have regrets related to my mother's death tormented me. Though people around me made every attempt to assure me it wasn't my fault. In my mind, if I had done things differently, she would still be here. Or that's just wishful thinking.

Throughout the year, Mom's focus was on making sure we had what we needed. Christmas time is when she made sure we had what we wanted. She reminded me of the holiday meme, "How moms look at their kids opening gifts on Christmas." The same proud face shown on the meme is what I remember my mom having year after year. Christmas was her favorite holiday. She would go all out. Nothing was off limits; we could get anything we wanted. This was before online shopping was an option. She would call stores to see if they had the items. She would go from store to store on

Chicago public transportation. That was the only time that price or location wasn't an obstacle.

Christmas of 1985 and 1986 were the most memorable for me. In 1985 I'd asked for the Matchbox Voltron. It was the top gift on my list. I knew my mom would deliver because she always did. When she told me that she tried to get it and couldn't, it was the worst feeling. I was so disappointed. She was so convincing. When I opened my gifts on Christmas, I was the happiest kid in the world. My mom made it happen! Christmas of 1986, I asked for a Nintendo with a Robot. She was determined to make sure I had it. She even had me calling stores to see if they had it. I didn't get it for Christmas. I was disappointed, but I knew she had tried. That following February, it was back in stock. It didn't matter that it wasn't Christmas anymore. My mom didn't hesitate to go and purchase it. That meant a lot to me. So much that I was the same way with my children as they grew up. Christmas was big in our house. Now that they have gotten older, I miss it. I miss her.

I miss her as my mom and my friend. She wasn't always my friend. I can still hear her voice, "I'm not your friend." Something said by Black mothers very often. She meant it. My mom did not play with kids. It was her way of creating boundaries with us. If she was always our mom, she would always remain in authority. We would never have to wonder if she was serious or not. She kept that standard until I was an adult. I remember the moment I knew our relationship was changing. I'd been dating the young lady that would eventually become my wife. I hadn't made any commitments and was still seeing other people. My mom was fond of my future wife and made it truly clear when I brought someone else home. My mom continuously switched up the names and, at one point, told me she was going to call my future wife and tell her that I had another girl at our house. I didn't find the humor in it, but my mother was so tickled. That's when I realized she had a sense of humor. Our friendship grew from there.

I could talk to my mother about everything. The night before the ambulance came, she and I were up talking for hours. For about a week, I'd been saying I was going to see her. Things kept coming up, and time was slipping by. Earlier that day, I was driving by her block and saw her outside putting up Christmas lights. I didn't stop by then, but later my wife told me that I needed to pick up my mother's prescription from Walgreens. When I dropped her medication off, I decided to stay and talk. I was there from 7 pm until about midnight. We had plenty of those conversations over the years. I had no idea that night would be our last. When I left, I told her I would be there to pick her up in the morning to take her to work. When she finally agreed, I went home.

She called me at about 3 am to come over. She said that when I got there, she needed me to call the ambulance. I wasn't alarmed because she sounded normal. I thought there was something wrong with my younger brother. I quickly got dressed and headed to her house. She lived four blocks away from me, so it didn't take me long. Something told me to call the ambulance before heading over, but I waited. When I got there, she was bent over on her dresser, gasping for air. Her lungs were collapsing. I called 9-1-1, but it felt like it took forever for the paramedics to come. When they arrived, they didn't intubate her. She'd stopped breathing at this point. The hospital closest to her house was at capacity, so they transported her to a hospital that was further away. The entire ride, the paramedics only used a manual resuscitator. By the time they got her to the hospital, she had died.

The emergency department staff worked on her and was able to revive her. However, there was a lack of oxygen in her brain for over eight minutes. The lack of an uninterrupted flow of oxygen to her brain caused her brain cells to deteriorate, causing her to go into a coma. My family felt like I'd done everything I could do. They told me I couldn't blame myself. But how could I not? I should have called the ambulance. If I had gone to see her when I could, I could have seen the signs. I was at the hospital every day. When I would go to work, I functioned as long as nobody talked to me. I was carrying the emotional weight of my mother's condition. If someone spoke to me, I couldn't stop crying. I was put on a leave of absence.

My mother was in a coma from December 4, 2000, until the day she died on March 30, 2001. After her funeral, I tried to get back into my routine, but emotionally I was tormented. The only thing that gave me relief was making music. It took me to another place. It was like a drug. I had to do it all the time. It was the only thing that took my mind off things. For years after that, I had that battle in my mind. So, I spent more time with my music and less time with my family. It got to the point where it became stress for my marriage. I wasn't emotionally stable.

In 2019, I started to realize I hadn't grieved my mother. All those years, I carried terrible baggage. I began to make sense of why things weren't working quite right for me. I held the sorrow and grief of feeling like everything that happened with my mom was my fault. It wasn't until last June that I was able to see where I went wrong in situations. I avoided my hurt by pouring myself into making music. In my second marriage, I tried to overcompensate for the failures of my first marriage. I functioned that way with my children as well. When I realized these unhealthy behaviors, I worked on forgiving myself. I lost a lot of years, consumed by my guilt and grief. Now I can live.

My Dandelion
E'a Williams

Ode To Dandelion

When we met, you were already on the cusp of giving up
(did I add to that grip in your gut),
We thought you were just into that Emo stuff,
kids are painting their nails black again,
Daria is on the television,
Kurt Kobain record playin',
Your beauty you couldn't see already
Double D's only in the 6th grade
awkward & afraid.
Your skin is a beautiful chocolate
but you weren't proud to rock it.
Your hair I would call good
but not in the hood
I loved it cuz it made the locs mine never could.
Sing any song & draw the album cover
to go along the beauty, you took from us
could go on & on...

We all agree there is a circle of life, and it includes death. We expect older people to pass on and can accept it a little better than an innocent person lost to gun violence or a child to cancer. We sometimes even pray for the death of a loved one who has been suffering from an illness or kept alive on a machine. We are grateful they are now at peace. But what our unconscious bias doesn't prepare us for is the feeling of anger and betrayal of your child lost to suicide. The anger at a child who you counseled for years about their depression and suicidal thoughts and talked away from the ledge. The anger at a child with who you shared your own feelings and agreed with theirs about this unfair life. The anger at a child with who you shared your own suicidal thoughts, hoping your stories of empathy would give them the strength to live on. The support through repeated scares and cries for help, through multiple failed attempts. The anger at a child you just spoke with and made plans with for that same weekend they chose to commit suicide. The anger at a child for being so selfish to do it during a time of celebration for the family, a baby shower, graduation, and her favorite little brother returning home from the summer at Yaya's house. You were his favorite sibling. The anger that you didn't give him at least one last good time to remember you by. The anger at a child who ignored your calls and kept standing you up as their decision became more real to them and maybe just maybe you were ignored because they knew your disappointment or maybe your power to talk them off the ledge one more time … and they didn't want that … they wanted death. The anger that you now took away any chance of me committing suicide because I can't do that to your little brother … again.

So, what exactly is suicide prevention when you've done all the things, and you've been all the things, and it still "failed." The betrayal of friends and family who didn't hold space for a stepmother to grieve because, after all, "She wasn't really your child so why you so upset." Maybe because I was even less than a stepmother because your father and I never got married, just shared a lot of life and your little brother. Not blood that made you my child, but the heart-filled years spent, the love given and received. The betrayal of God to let such a beautiful and talented spirit be taken by the pain this world has to offer and not honor my prayers and faithfulness.

I remember when we went on a healing walk one day, and you commented on all the "dead" dandelions blowing through the air. It really did look like we were in a snow globe. We grabbed them and made whimsical wishes to time travel and for magical unicorn horns, purple skin, and fairy wings. I explained to you then that in their death they are actually bringing new life. Those are actually seeds blowing through the air. Still, in your macabre state of mind, you whispered under your breath, "I'll be a dandelion then." I playfully punched you and said I'd bring you back from the dead and kill you myself if you ever took yourself from me. You grabbed my hand, assured me you loved me, and we walked hand in hand in silence back to the house.

I don't think time can ever heal such a wound ... you just learn to live with it. It's been three years, and it still feels like yesterday. I still window shop for you and want to invite you to things that only we would enjoy together because our square never fit in the circles, which is why we got along so well. I can't go through certain parts of town without pushing back tears, if I can travel through them at all. I forget and sometimes still try and give you a call.

Promising to not let you die in vain, understanding how trying to live in this world was just too much for the both of us, I will not give up. You are my Dandelion!

It Doesn't End

Eden Voigt

I remember the day he died in pieces. I didn't know it would
be a day of significance, so most of that day was a blur. It was
July 17, and it must have been after five because my mom
worked until then, at least. She got home and came into my
room asking if I had heard from my dad recently. I replied that
I hadn't. A look of worry washed over her face. I could tell
she thought the worst had happened. She wanted to go check
on him and asked if I would come with her. My sister had
friends over that evening, so they stayed home.

My mom was rushing me out of the house, and I thought she
must be overreacting. "My dad just has the flu—he is fine," I
thought. He was supposed to take my sister and me that
weekend, but he had been ill for a few days.

As we were driving down the street, a thought that I am sure
had already occurred to my mom dawned on me—my dad
could be dead. I quickly pushed this thought aside as if it were
completely insane because it just did not seem possible. I
knew my father had struggled with substance abuse issues
since college and, in particular, alcohol. Despite knowing this
about him, I still could not conceive of him being gone. At
this point in my life, I had not dealt with a lot of death. It did
not feel real and still doesn't today.

We got to his house but no answer. My mom picked up a rock
and threw it at his bedroom window but still nothing. I spotted
a neighbor looking at us from his back porch.

"Is everything okay? Do you need some help?" he shouted
across his barren yard.

"My ex-husband won't answer the door—we're really worried about him," my mom replied.

He came over to help us try to get a response from my dad. After a few minutes of nothing, he suggested we call the police to do a wellness check.

We could hear his dog barking from the apartment, yet he still wasn't answering his phone or responding to the rocks thrown at his window. At that moment, I prayed he was just out at the grocery store and his phone was broken. It wasn't rational thinking, but I would choose to believe it, rather than hat he was not okay.

We made our way back to the car, and my mom called the police for a welfare check. They were not quick to get to his house, and when they did, they were not helpful. They tried convincing my mom and me that he had probably just gone on a trip for the weekend.

"That's not possible. He would have told us and there is absolutely no way he would have left his dog here!" my mom refuted.

"Okay, just calm down, ma'am," said the officer.

I don't remember what happened after that. I stayed in the car playing a game on my iPod while my mom told the officers about my dad's substance abuse problems, how he had been sick, and that they would need to break down the door. They must have eventually, but all I remember is my mom bursting out of the door of his building a few moments later. Tears consumed her face, and she screamed as I had never heard her do before. At that moment, I knew what had happened. I swung the car door open, and she went in for a hug, but her knees buckled beneath her, and we both fell to the ground. I don't remember what words she used, but I do remember saying, "He won't see me graduate. He won't see me get married. He won't be there for any of it."

The rest of the evening is all melted together. Eventually, we got home. There were a lot of phone calls and tears.

I can't remember the days after. At his funeral, I couldn't give my speech, so a family friend read it for me. The room was completely full, and we had run out of chairs. Yes, my father had his issues—as we all do—but he was a good person and an amazing father.

When I went back to school in the fall, nobody knew what to say, so they said nothing. I can't blame them for that. I don't know if I would have acted differently if it happened to someone else, but it didn't happen to someone else. I became extremely isolated after that. It was not a healthy way to cope, and I don't recommend it. Even in the years following, I struggled immensely. I lost some of my best friends, and in turn, I became introverted and started to hate the world. I lost my social skills, and everyday interactions were difficult. Eventually, I began high school, and it was... well, a disaster. I loathed every second of my time at that school.

I convinced my mom to let me do a year of online school, and it was challenging in different ways. After my sophomore year, I returned to school in person, and things began to pick up. I formed a solid group of friends who cared about me and helped me get through the days. I didn't do this on my own, though. I had been in therapy for years at this point, and though it took me a while to find the right therapist for me, it really does make a difference.

At times it's felt like it would never ever feel better, and this will sound corny, but it is true in my experience—time heals. It hurts to admit, but my memory of my father has faded—not entirely, of course, but it has faded. I try not to blame myself for this since I only had 11 full years with him, and now, I am nearly 19. It doesn't hurt less because the memories have faded, though—the wound is healing because of the time I have had to process it. I talk to my siblings and my mom about my dad—his funny quirks and strange likes and dislikes. We talk about his childish sense of humor and the shyness that was with him even into his forties.

I have dealt with more deaths since his, and I am sure I will only deal with more. After all, a part of life is death and grief. Soon after his death, my dog died unexpectedly, then my uncle, then my dad's mom, and most recently, my dad's brother. It is not as though death becomes any less tragic, but for me, it has become less scary. Death no longer feels like the end. I know it can't be —after all, energy cannot be destroyed, just merely transferred from one form into another. That realization has comforted me in the times when I feel hopelessly sad. It stops the flow of tears and gives air to my lungs, allowing me to take a deep breath. I think about my father every day. Sometimes it's in the morning and sometimes right before I go to sleep, but I think about him every day. I miss him deeply, and at one time, I felt as though I could not go on. I could not think of a future without him in it, so then I could not envision a future with me in it. That time and those feelings have passed because I know my dad wants me to continue. He wants me to go to college and graduate. He wants me to be happy and loved. Grief does not end, but it changes stages. I still grieve for my father, and I think I always will, but I can, and I will live my life.

Empty Seat
Alea Allen

I became a teacher with the desire and intention to make a difference in the lives of students who are often overlooked and unheard of. My ambition was to expose my students to not only the content area of academics but also the content of my heart. I wanted them to learn their value in this world by creating a loving and inviting atmosphere for them to be free to embrace not only who they entered the classroom as but also who they aspired to become.

I've had the honor and privilege of being an educator for 20 years. Sixteen of those years I taught in Chicago at six public schools within low socio-economic neighborhoods. My students endured multiple traumas, from gang violence to child abuse, rape, and death, but they knew that my room was a haven. They could come to me about anything without judgment or ridicule. Accountability? Yes, but never any judgment, regardless of the circumstances. I think one of the things that cultivated such a strong bond between my students and me is the fact that I shared a lot of their experiences, but I also wanted them to know that their circumstances didn't have to define them or defeat them. But death can not only make you feel defeated, it has the capacity to destroy your spirit.

Over the course of my tenure as a teacher, I have lost 13 students. You know, when you enter the classroom for the first time, everyone talks to you about preparing kids for assessments and making sure that you teach the standards, but no one mentors you on the pain and anguish associated with the loss of a child. It literally knocks the wind out of you.

No one prepares you for the knock on a classroom door by a security guard to inform you that one of your students has been killed when, in fact, he was supposed to be in your classroom at the time. No one tells you that one day there will be a kid who tried his hardest to get back in school, but because of his behavior, he was turned away and led back to the streets. The very place he so desperately tried to escape is the very place that took his life. The college preparatory courses for academic pedagogy do not prepare you to endure the loss of a student in a tragic car accident over Christmas break, and instead of assembling for graduation, to gather with his classmates for a tribute. No one forewarns you about the empty seat and the name of a child who has departed from life on earth still being on the roster. No one gives you the words to say when you lose a student and her brother, who is also your student, shows up to class the next day devastated and broken. My students were my rock. We supported each other through our hurt and pain. Some people have advised me not to get close to my students in order to avoid the sting of losing them to the streets, jail, or the grave, but if I did that, I would fail at doing what God called me to do, which is to *love* them.

Death is one of the most crippling and devastating encounters life presents to us, and no one is exempt from its reach. Thirteen of my babies have left this earth due to death's grasp, and each one tore a piece of me. While each loss has left holes in my heart, the departure of Son Son shattered my spirit. This young man was a light that illuminated any room with his smile. He could lighten an intense moment with his quirky laugh and sense of humor. All the girls loved him, and the guys wanted to be like him. He was my baby boy, though. He faced so many challenges in life and his senior year was the most challenging, with the loss of his best friend and the complications straddling the hold of the streets and the calling on his life. Son Son was shot in the stomach in December of 2013, and he had his mother call me from the hospital. I was so grateful that he survived and that he knew that I loved him dearly. I just wish that there was something that I could have done to prevent the beast that was waiting for him in the nine months to follow.

Our last encounter was through text messages early one Saturday morning.

Son Son: "Hey ma"

Me: "Who is this?"

Son Son: "Your oldest son."

Me: "Hey, Son! How are you? What have you been up to?"

Son Son: "Ma, I'm just trying to stay alive."

Why should any child have to worry about staying alive? Son Son was snatched away from this world on September 6, 2014, and with him, he took a chunk of my heart and a piece of my soul.

BUT GOD! GOD IS THE REDEEMER OF ALL!

Losing Son Son cut me to my core, in conjunction with the deaths that preceded his and those that followed, but God never left me. He was and is my comforter. God reassured me that there's purpose in my pain and in the pain of so many others who endure loss. As a teacher, I often reflect on how to improve lessons and strategies, and I wish that I had the opportunity to do something different, be the teacher I am now for my babies that aren't here anymore. I wonder if there's anything that could have changed the trajectory of their lives. That's the human side of all of us, to ponder the possibilities.

BUT GOD!

I'm thankful that God chose me to be in each of the schools that were assigned to me. I'm blessed to have developed such beautiful and lasting relationships with my students. The impact that I sought to make on their lives is nothing compared to the imprint that they have left on my heart.

A New Plan

Luke Lucas

I was born a caretaker. My mom was two weeks shy of 50 when she had me. My dad was 52. I had three brothers, but the one closest in age to me was already 22. I was not a planned baby. Both of my parents were in declining health and having a newborn did not help. My mom bore the physical trauma of childbirth at 50 in 1980, when medical care was not what it is today. My dad had developed a heart condition through a childhood illness, had been wounded in World War II, and had diabetes. I watched them both die slow, painful deaths. On the outside, I looked like I managed it well. On the inside, I let the pain and depression ruin me.

When I was nine years old, my dad had his second major open-heart surgery in a decade. He was a tough guy and survived it. But the staph infection he contracted from the surgery shut his body down in stages. He lost the will to live. A few days before he died, he had finally made it home from the hospital. Why he was discharged, I'll never know. But his fever had gotten so high that he turned the air conditioner on, opened up all the windows, and slumped in his favorite chair. That's how my mom and I found him when we got home from school. It looked like that scene from the original Avengers movie when The Hulk takes Loki and smashes him over and over again on the floor. Loki is a comic book character, so he just moaned and asked for a drink. My dad looked broken.

That's a look into how I process that trauma. My dad died in May of 1990. I see him in a movie in 2012. My imagination always makes connections back to trauma. Are you ever up late at night? You've seen those ads for lawyers filing class action lawsuits for victims of mesothelioma. That's a lung condition you get from, among other things, inhaling asbestos. When my dad was in one hospital, crews wore full hazmat suits while they removed the original insulation for the building: asbestos. The trauma even taints the Bee Gees. My dad loved the bass line from "Stayin' Alive." I mean, a lot of people do. It slaps. But I always remember my mom telling me he used to push the needle back on the stereo so it would just play the bass line over and over again. Whenever I hear it, I think of him.

Trauma is cruel because it takes this priority line straight to the middle of your brain. He was alive for eight years of my life. His sense of humor was wild. He was always proud of my schoolwork and taped my tests to his wall. When we would play frisbee, and he got tired, he'd whip it up on the roof of our apartment building and say, "Whoops! I don't know what happened. Game's over!" I can be funny because of him. I can say someone was proud of me because he was. I learned how to be passive-aggressive from him. (Maybe that's not great, but he did it in style.) But I really have to think to produce those memories. They get washed out and replaced by the memory of watching him slowly die.

The trauma blocks out the good times. When I block out the trauma, it's like erasing him completely. That's bone-chilling to me.

My dad's ultimate illness lasted four months. For a nine-year-old, that's a legit eternity. I spent many evenings in ICU waiting rooms with nothing to do but wait. Is he getting better? Is he coming home? Is he dead yet? That was nothing compared to my mom's death. She started to get really ill about six months after my dad died. It was right after I turned ten. My mom died right after I turned 26.

Mom had high blood pressure her whole life but got it under control. She was overweight, so she lost 100 pounds. She smoked for 54 years and quit cold turkey. My mom fought back. Eventually, though, illness won. There was an abscessed tooth that limited her communication and fired infection throughout her blood. She developed macular degeneration, which puts huge blurry patches in all but your peripheral vision. There were multiple mini-strokes that compromised her cognitive abilities. From those, she developed dementia, which was truly scary. There were also heart issues, which led to the thing that killed her: lung cancer.

So that's a whole lot. My dad was dead, and my brothers had their own lives. I became the caretaker and eventually the breadwinner for both of us. When you're 10 and 11 years old, it's really difficult not to be able to talk to your mom for days because saying something like "Hello" could cause a massive toothache. Because she also didn't want me to leave the house, I stayed home, got fat, and watched a ton of TV. This was before cell phones, computers, or any Wu-Tang albums came out. It was boring.

I became a sad, isolated young man that looked for the bad to happen. No one ever tried to help out. I figured I was on my own. People would come to visit or "hear things." What they saw would make them ask if I loved my mom. They asked if I cared about what people were saying. I was seventeen. I was not set up to be the caretaker. And no one "heard anything." They got calls from my mom asking for help. And neither of us got any.

In the real world, where real people live, I did the best I could. In my head, where I've spent most of my life, I was the bad son who caused all my mom's pain. It spun me out into a limbo where I never really did anything for myself. I felt better being a caretaker in any form possible. Springtime became hard for me. It's a time of renewal, but I'd see other people's lives moving forward while mine stayed the same. There were three reasons for that. That was what I was raised to expect out of life. The anxiety and raging obsessive-compulsive disorder I had developed kept me afraid of living. And I felt I deserved it for being a bad person.

The sad caretaker is the life I lived. At my job, I've taken on an incredible amount of responsibility in a toxic environment. And I never left that job. It's as if I'm afraid to give up on it, like I gave up on my mom. Sure, I'm now well paid as a system director for a national health care company. But I have little support. When I did try to do something fun, I ruined it. I did a lot of improv. That's comedy made up on the spot, on stage, with other people. Everyone would always say that they felt taken care of when I was their scene partner. What went unspoken was the part where I was too afraid to move the scene forward on my own. That put a lot of pressure on everyone else and made me a welcomed but tiring scene partner.

As wrong as it may be, I had to admit the blame I placed on myself. I had to admit what it had done to me. No one can just blow that off. I felt that blame into existence. So, I had to forgive myself. It's not a rubbing your hands together, clapping, and walking away type of forgiveness. I had to address that I was just a kid in a tough situation. I was not perfect. I shouldn't have expected to be perfect. It's ok for me to move on. I've only just started that process, and I'm 40. The sun burns a little hotter when you come out of that fog to realize you're giving yourself permission to live when you're already getting old.

If I started a family now, what if my kids have to nurse me?

What if my wife ends up being a single mom?

What if I just create more broken people?

Those "what if's" were my way of keeping myself down. The anxiety and OCD are real, but I felt refuge in the way they kept me insulated from getting my feelings hurt. Once I admitted these mechanisms were in place and that I built them, I could acknowledge them and slowly let them go. That is truly processing the trauma. I spent a long time feeling all the wrong feelings. It's not easy. I'm only just beginning that process, so there's no reveal about how much better I've gotten with bouncy examples. One huge positive I can give you: As I've let go and moved on, I accept that I'm a halfway decent person. I deserve happiness and love. I'm not demanding it. I'm just becoming a person who is able to accept it. I was not a planned baby. Why would I live like my life was planned to be entirely trauma and grief? I don't know why anymore. And I don't intend to look back for that answer.

I'll Take an Argument

As told by Monique Jackson

I would take an argument right about now, anything to hear his voice again. Sometimes when I close my eyes, I can hear him. I can hear every octave of his voice because I have been listening to it for years.

The voice that belongs to the love of my life,

my best friend,

my daughter's father,

my husband,

my everything,

for so many years.

There will never be any new material. Only recordings I keep in my head of the numerous conversations we've had.

I remember meeting him. I was visiting family for a funeral. I remember having an engaging conversation with him at a family member's home. He seemed to be a genuine person; I had no idea that he may have been flirting with me. I stepped away to go to the restroom, and when I came out, he was standing there. He was waiting to make his move. A little creepy, but it was flattering. He gave me his number and asked me to give him a ring sometime. A few weeks went by before I called him.

Talking to him was so easy. We talked on the phone for hours. Our conversation continued to bloom until we had a beautiful garden of colorful conversations. We talked about so much that there were no limits. Time froze when we would talk. We started to develop a fantastic long-distance friendship. It developed naturally. Our conversations went from getting to know each other to knowing everything about one another. We went beyond introducing our dating persona. We presented ourselves raw and uncut. Being that open at the beginning allowed for empathy later in the relationship.

He was a different kind of person. I remember being in a car accident that required me to have surgery. I was nervous about the surgery and knew that recovery would be challenging. When I was released from the hospital, I had to stay with my family. The comfort of my own home would have been preferred, but I needed all the help I could get. I couldn't get around on my own. I was forever grateful, but there is something about being at home. I expressed that a lot when talking to him. One day, as I was sitting around, I looked up and he was there. I asked him what he was doing here. I can still hear him say, "I came to take you home." I knew then that he would always take care of me.

He always took care of my daughter and me. I was a single mom when I met him. The environment with her father was unfavorable for our emotional health. I was incredibly determined when I left that relationship that I couldn't and wouldn't go back to anything that looked even remotely like that again. I made that clear with Mr. Jackson before getting seriously involved. A peaceful home is a priority. He heard me, and we were safe with him. The way he stepped in as a father figure to my daughter made my heart smile. I remember him sitting and doing homework with her with such patience. Way more than I had. He didn't have any biological children but had a paternal nature. Until the day he left this earth, Mr. Jackson was her father. He loved her and made many decisions based on what would be suitable for her. That was honorable in my eyes.

Mr. Jackson loved him some me! We had a special relationship. Everyone knew how we felt about one another. The intimacy that we shared went beyond the physical. He was my soul mate. I don't know any other way to describe the love that we shared. We were in sync about most things. Religion wasn't one of them. That made me hesitate before entering an exclusive relationship with him. I am a Christian, and he was a Muslim. I'd always pictured myself being with someone in the same faith as me. There is a scripture that talks about a house being divided against itself, not standing. It concerned me, but we worked. I was open to something new with him. Being upfront about the concerns and having mutual respect for one another's faith was imperative. It did not create the challenge that I thought it would. We were working.

Being with Mr. Jackson had more ups than downs. Yet the downs were low and hurtful. Mr. Jackson and his mother were so alike that sometimes they bumped heads. When she wasn't around, he was peaceful. However, if she was around, there was this other side of him that was hard to describe. I wasn't used to seeing it. They weren't good together. I noticed this early on, but it was undeniable when she had to live with us for a while. He turned into another person. Not only towards her but also me. I knew that something had to change. Once we were separated from her, it was better, until it wasn't.

Mr. Jackson and I did not have a perfect relationship. It was our genuine love for one another that carried us through those challenging moments. Then came a time that love wasn't enough. Mr. Jackson and I had hit a rough patch, and I'd lost all my fight. I told him it would be best that we separate. He wasn't happy about it. I'd gone away for the weekend with our daughter, and when we returned, there was a For Sale sign in the yard. I know I said we would separate but to put it on the market that quickly was beyond me. His response was if we weren't going to be here, why would he keep the house. I had to quickly find a place to live. I am reminded of the phrase, "Hurt people, hurt people." Mr. Jackson was hurt and responded in a revengeful way. This is why I wasn't willing to reconcile when he reached out around Thanksgiving of that year.

Why would I go back to someone who was the reason my daughter and I were homeless? How do you go from loving us and my daughter being your world to not caring if we had a safe, warm place to lay our heads? Even though I knew this was a reaction to his hurt, I was now hurt and not willing to take him back. I didn't stop loving him. I just couldn't believe my husband had treated me like this. Following that conversation was a very different one, it was not with him but about him.

He'd been visiting family for the holidays and had gotten sick. COVID-19 had attacked his body, and he wasn't improving. I was notified of his condition and traveled to see him. I couldn't believe that the vibrant man I'd grown to love wasn't able to greet me when I walked into the hospital room.

Couldn't respond to me calling his name.

Couldn't smile at the sight of me.

Couldn't tell me everything was going to be ok.

I wonder if he even knew I was there. The hurt my heart felt at the thought of this being the end was overwhelming. Why didn't I just take him back?

I played the dangerous "What if" game with myself. We could have gotten back together, and he would have been with me for the holidays. He'd still be here. Why couldn't I just put my pride to the side? He was sorry. Why didn't I just forgive him? I've struggled every day with this. His death is still fresh for me, and so are my hurt and regret. I miss him so much. We've been apart before, but at least then I could call and hear his voice even if it wasn't a pleasant conversation. My options are gone now. I will never be able to argue with Mr. Jackson again.

My Brother
Marissa McPherson

The first time I ever dealt with grief was when my uncle passed away. Uncle Damon was my favorite and couldn't anybody tell me anything wrong about him. I remember the day as if it were yesterday. The night before he went to surgery, I asked him if he was scared, and he told me "No," he would be fine. When, my mom told me she had something to tell me, I knew exactly what she would say. I turned around and walked out of the house, angry at God because I didn't understand why he took someone that I loved so dearly away from me. I was angry, hurt, and in disbelief. He was like my best friend. I didn't have a father growing up, so he was the closest thing to it. I can remember going to his house during the summer and hanging out with him and my cousins. I can still remember him greeting us as we walked through the door or seeing him sit in his backyard having a beer. I can remember running around and playing, or even when we got in trouble, how he would fuss at us. When he passed, everything changed. We no longer went to his house, and we no longer spent time with my family, and to this day, all of that hurts. Other family members passed before, but now I was old enough to understand. I will never see him again. I remember sitting at the funeral and hearing the screams of my cousins and blaming God for everything. I can only imagine what my family and my life would be like if he was still here. Suppose my boys had a chance to meet such a great person. If only he had made it through the surgery. That gave me a different outlook on life. I thought nothing in life could ever hurt me again until I lost my brother back in 2019.

Losing my brother Tony was a different kind of pain. Growing up I thought I only had one sister, and then at the age of 16, I found out I had seven other siblings—it completely blew my mind. I remember another brother messaging me on social media, saying, "Is he yo real daddy?" Tony and I went to the same school for a year and never knew each other. We grew up in the same town and never knew that we had each other. I regret not making more time with him while he was here. To hear his family share memories, they have of him growing up breaks my heart because I never had a chance to make those memories. We would talk on the phone often, and I can still hear his voice and his advice. He worked overnight, and I would call him just to bug him. He would be so upset because I would be out doing something I shouldn't. It was out of love because he wanted the best for me. He would encourage me to do better and be a great mom. But it hurts that I don't have many memories of him. My son cries because he does not understand why his uncle Tony is not here. I try not to think about this a lot because I want to be strong for our family. Deep down, it's eating me up inside.

I don't understand how people go to a grave site and sit as if the person is there.

You can't touch them.

You can't smell them.

You can't see them.

At 31, I don't understand grief, and I don't think I fully understand death. All I know is that it comes with a lot of pain and confusion. I've attended plenty of funerals, and I've cried many times, but this pain in my heart, I don't think, will ever go away. I would call Tony so upset and frustrated with my dad, even when I was having boy trouble—he was always there. He always gave excellent advice. He never missed my son's birthday parties, and he was a fantastic father. I look at his photos and try to just remember the few memories I do have. His smile, his face, and the things he would say to me.

It only took cancer a few months to take him. As much as I tried to encourage my family to trust in God, it was tough for me to do. I'd go to the hospital on my lunch break. I'd never watched someone slowly die. I could see him declining. He looked different. The things he was saying, and his hallucinations were overwhelming.

I got a call while at work, and my dad said to get to the hospital because he wouldn't make it through the night. I ran out, praying to God to keep him here. I selfishly asked if God didn't do anything else for my family to just keep him here. At the time, I didn't think I was selfish for thinking like that, but now I know I was. At the hospital, everyone was trying to say their final goodbyes and looking at him. The cancer had ravished his body, and he didn't look like himself. I never realized what cancer could really do to a person. And then he was gone. I wanted to scream, and I wanted to yell at the doctors because I felt like it was their job to fix this, but all I could do was cry.

At his funeral, I was dreaming. We got to his burial site. His mother's scream, as his body was lowered to the ground made everything real. I was utterly torn inside.

I never thought he would be gone.

I never thought I wouldn't be able to see him again.

I never thought I wouldn't be able to hear his laugh.

I really miss my brother.

My William

As told by Tracy Cruz

Two things happen when I hear or say his name, either a
schoolgirl smile or tears. Sometimes both, sometimes it starts
as a smile and ends in tears. Either way, William is now a
bittersweet subject for me. It feels like my right hand has been
cut off. Like many amputees, the most visible effect is the loss
itself. My William is no longer here. I will never wake him in
the morning. I will never know he is in the room with a simple
inhale. I will never walk into an event with him behind me. I
will never wake William up again. Without him, I am forced
to function differently. I am forced to learn to adjust to life,
minus one. I also occasionally suffer from phantom limb pain.
Feeling like he is here just to be snatched back into reality.
William is gone. I didn't see it coming.

To say that William was the love of my life would be an
understatement. I was his world, and he was mine. We
enjoyed one another. Our lives were woven together like a
cord of three strands: God, William, and me. Eventually, our
two dogs made our family complete. We had a bond that
couldn't be broken. I remember us having a conversation once
about what would happen if one of us died. He said with such
confidence, "You are the only woman for me. I would never
remarry." He showed it! William was a kind person, but if you
had issues with his wife, he had nothing to do with you.

In the summer of 2020, after a few doctor visits, we learned
that I was having some health challenges and would need to
have surgery. William remained by my side. He'd taken some
time off work to be with me during recovery. We spent the
2020 holidays together. When I was well enough to be
without him, he went back on the road. He returned once
more, but it was the last time he would leave for a job.
William would say things like, "I'm not a truck driver. Driving

is my job." I am not 100% sure what it meant, but I am guessing he was reassuring me that the road was not his home. His home was here with me. So, when I learned that William was having trouble breathing and was going from urgent care to the emergency room, I thought he'd get better and come home.

When I was traveling to Virginia to be with him, I sincerely believed we'd be coming home together. I was recently asked if I thought William prepared me to live without him. The truth is, I didn't necessarily need to be prepared to live without him. He was a truck driver and would be gone for extended periods of time. I was used to him being gone, but he always came home. There was a sense of security in knowing that even though I was alone today, I wasn't lonely because the love of my life would be home soon. This time William didn't come home. This time the goodbye was final. There will be no more hugs, no more kisses, no more support, no more companionship, no more laughs, no more holidays, no more good times, no more challenging times. I'm still trying to wrap my mind around it, but I do understand that no matter how much time I spend thinking about it, the circumstances of my husband's death will not change.

As a truck driver, Williams traveled all over the United States. This trip to Iowa was supposed to be quick. After the drop, he was supposed to come back home. However, the company rerouted him to Virginia. When he got there, he was already sick. Upon arriving at the emergency room, his chest x-rays were "bad," and the doctors wanted to treat him for COVID-19, even though he'd not yet been diagnosed. After a few days of being in the hospital, medical professionals decided that his breathing was getting worse, and he'd need to be put on a ventilator. William was not happy about that and was giving the staff a hard time. He was refusing to be placed on a ventilator, but I had the opportunity to talk to him. With a little wifely persuading, he calmed down and agreed. We each said, "I love you." That was the last time I would hear him say it. I made my way to Virginia, and I'm grateful to God that the process was smooth. I traveled with his best friend in the middle of a snowstorm. Or should I say a snowstorm was going on *around* us. It never touched us. It was like the Lord was parting the Red Sea for me to get to my husband. When I arrived in Virginia, I was able to book a hotel that was only 10 minutes from the hospital. This was at the height of COVID-19, so generally, family members weren't allowed to visit loved ones in hospitals. I was allowed to stay with him every day. I couldn't be in the room with him, but I could see him through the glass. He was able to hear my voice over the phone. At some point, I sprayed perfume on a washcloth, and the nurse took it to him. He was able to smell my scent and know that I was there.

Seventeen days, two hours, and thirty-eight minutes is how long my William lasted with COVID-19 in the hospital. During that time, and while making funeral arrangements, I was numb. I'd never been the primary person responsible for planning a funeral. I learned so much in the process. From working with a funeral home in Virginia to having William shipped to Georgia to making sure a Georgia funeral home was there to receive him. I received extraordinarily little compassion from some people. Everyone was focused on money. It was bad enough trying to process the death of my William, but on top of that, I had to make all these plans I was not mentally and emotionally prepared to make.

I made it through his funeral. Barely. When it was all over, and I had time to think, I realized I'd been robbed. Robbed of my William, of my best friend, of my husband. Death came like a thief in the night. Death brings grief. They are companions. They grab hold of you and take you on a ride that you didn't sign up for. I've experienced bumps and bruises while processing William's death. Including the deaths of my father and stepfather within months of my

William. I've felt hurt, anger, disbelief, sadness, loneliness, regret, blame, acceptance, and peace. It hasn't been easy. The joy and love God blessed me with felt snatched from me. I've made every effort to stay strong and endure. I fight daily to not be consumed by all my grief.

Oh, Mama

Anonymous

I had been preparing for this day since I was twelve. My grandmother always seemed old to me. She was like 62 and I tried to mentally prepare myself for her to die. Back then, everyone seemed old, and if you were in your sixties, I couldn't imagine you being any older. I guessed after turning 65, everyone would just automatically turn into a corpse. Obviously, that didn't happen, so as I got older, we got closer and closer. She was like a mother to me—like a traditional TV mom, except she cussed. She cooked dinner, she made lunches, she fixed breakfast, she helped with homework, and she entertained us. Especially me because I was the youngest. She taught me how to gamble. She was my therapist and was always there to listen whenever I needed to talk. She always encouraged me whenever I wanted to do something. Bizarre stuff that nobody else would ever encourage me to do. Like if I told my grandmother I wanted to be a circus clown, she would say to me, "Go for it."

I got a call from my daughter, who told me that she had forgotten her book bag or jacket or something, so she went back home to get it and found my grandmother in the bed struggling to breathe. She asked me what to do. I told her to call 911 and to let me talk to my grandmother. I can still hear the conversation clearly. She seemed so nervous and confused. This was unfamiliar to her. And even if this was the end, she had been preparing for it for years. My grandmother went through a time when she just gave away everything. Anything she thought was of value. She just gave it away, any money she had, any secrets she had, she just gave away. I guess as she got older, she wanted to make sure that everything was taken care of when that day came.

"I don't know what to do," Mama said.

"What do you mean?"

She said, "I can't breathe, but I just, I don't know what to do. The firefighters are here, and I just, I don't know what to do."

At first, I didn't know what she was getting at. It was pretty cut and dry to me. "Go with the firemen to the hospital." But, to her, it was a big dilemma.

To her, it may be the end, and she didn't want to die in the hospital. She would talk to us about death a lot (mainly me), preparing for it, accepting it, and even embracing it since it is inevitable. She would tell me that she wanted to go in her sleep. She wanted to die at home, not at a hospital and certainly not "hooked up to all those tubes." So, at this moment, she was trying to decide if she wanted to basically drown to death at home because her lungs were full of fluid or go to the hospital and risk dying there. She told me because I would understand, and I did. If I knew there was no hope, I would have rushed over to sit with her and watch her go. But since we didn't know for sure what was going on, I told her, "YOU BETTER GO TO THE HOSPITAL!"

I don't know if she wasn't quite ready to die or if she wasn't expecting it to happen so suddenly. We were told she had heart failure a couple of months prior, and at her age, even if surgery was possible, no one wanted that for her. So, we were preparing for a gradual decline over several months or even years. That was just our wishful thinking. I suppose that the idea of death and actually facing it are totally different. Naturally, she went to the hospital. She usually listened to me when I forcefully suggested that she do something. They stabilized her in the ambulance and then proceeded to take her to the hospital.

She stayed in the hospital for a few days. My grandmother loved to socialize, so even though she didn't want to be in the hospital, I know she enjoyed the company. Due to her condition, she was given oxygen to help her breathe. She was supposed to relax, but that woman couldn't stop talking if there was anyone around to listen. We reminded her several times throughout her stay in the hospital to relax and stop talking so much, but she didn't. The sarcasm, jokes, and stories never stopped. After about three days, her doctor said the fluid on her lungs was gone; her oxygen level was back to an acceptable amount. She was instructed to set up an appointment with the pharmacist to adjust her medication, so this wouldn't happen again, and we took her home.

We took her to my mother's house because my grandmother's apartment was on the 3rd floor, and we all decided that she needed to stay with my mom until she got a little stronger, and then we would decide what she should do next. The night she came from the hospital, we were so happy, as if we had dodged a bullet. We spent the following day with her, listening to the many jokes she always had. I was getting ready to leave. She was using the bathroom, and she called me into the bathroom with her. She wanted to have a "toilet talk," which I felt was so weird. She wanted to look me in the face and tell me goodbye before I left.

Looking back, she had to know that she was telling me goodbye for the last time before she left to go to her eternal home. I usually shy away from weird interactions with people. Like when I was 12, my great aunt was terminally ill, and we went to see her before she made her transition. My grandmother "whispered" loudly, "She smells like pee. Go give her a hug." I already hated any kind of touching or affection, and then she told me that the woman smelled like pee!? When we went to walk out, I smiled, and my aunt leaned in to hug me. I knew after the fact that she heard my grandmother's loud whisper. But I kept walking, and I didn't know how to react to that. Should I go back or what? I didn't go back, and that replayed in my mind for years because I couldn't change it. So, when my grandmother wanted to have her "toilet talk," I just went in there and listened.

I had no idea this was going to be the last time I saw her. I got a call from my mom early the following day that my grandmother had passed away in her sleep. My mom said she thought something was wrong because she didn't hear her go to the bathroom in the middle of the night, and when she went upstairs to check on her, she was gone. I imagined she was overjoyed. She was reunited with her husband, her parents, all of her eight siblings, a boatload of friends, and extended family. I imagined she was fussing at the angels that came to get her "Shit, what took y'all so long?" I imagined if she could tell us anything to comfort us, she would say, "Hell, did you think I was gonna live forever?"

Looking at her pictures and realizing that she isn't here with me, hurts. It's hard to handle at times. I miss her so much. It's hard to describe in words. Then, other times I think about the things she said and the times we had together, and I appreciate that time so much, I can only feel grateful. I had an extraordinary grandmother for 36 years. I learned countless lessons and had some of the most memorable experiences because of this woman's life. Of all the people in the world to experience her greatness in the way I did, God chose to put us together. I miss her so much sometimes, but I don't feel bad anymore because I had 36 years of wonderful.

Early Grief

Tina Dillard

I remember being introduced to death and grief at an early age. I was maybe 9 or 10. We were all asleep when the telephone rang late at night at my grandmother's house. After he hung up the phone, my uncle burst into my room and yelled, "Mick John and Max got shot!" My heart started beating fast. I knew what that could mean, but it didn't hit me. A few hours later, my family learned that my 14-year-old cousin Mick John had died from a gunshot wound to the neck. My brother survived with a gunshot wound to the knee.

Because he was a star basketball player at his middle school, Mick John was very popular for his age. He was looking forward to playing as a freshman in high school. I remember him always smiling and carrying a basketball all the time. I believe he was good enough to go to the NBA one day. But a short walk from a friend's house changed our lives forever.

Mick John, whose real name is Thomas Weathersby, and my brother Max were very close. Our parents are siblings, so we grew up together. Mick and Max were both 14 years old. They loved video games but playing basketball together was their favorite. We lived in two different parts of the city. Both parts were heavy with gang violence. Max would visit Mick some weekends, and Mick would visit us. He was our brother from another mother. I ohad sleepovers with Mick John's little sister, Toya.

We were all nervous because Max was still in the hospital. He didn't know that his best friend was gone. Max asked about Mick. Seeing my brother get the news that Mick had died was tough. Watching him deal with the pain in his body and now his heart.

After this horrible incident, I was scared for my brother's life and angry that my cousin was killed. We all wanted to know who did this to our family and were sad because Mick John wasn't here anymore. We now had to live with the fact that he wouldn't be visiting us on the weekends and in the summertime anymore.

We had seen and heard about it happening to other families we knew, but this time it was our family. It was at our front door this time.

Mick John's funeral was my first.

It was scary seeing him in the casket.

He looked like he was sleeping.

All of his friends and teachers were there from school. Everyone was crying and consoling each other. We were in so much pain. We couldn't believe this had happened to Mick. He was such a good kid. He was nice to everyone. How could this happen to Mick John? He didn't bother people. Everyone loved him, and now he was gone. I remember walking out in the processional line to the grave site. Seeing Toya, his sister, down in a corner, hugging her knees. I could only stare because I didn't know what to say to her.

My brother was alive, and hers wasn't.

I remember I didn't want her to be upset with me because of that.

I stopped going to visit Toya. The shooting happened down the street from their house. That made me sad. We moved to Mississippi because my grandmother feared for my brother's life. She felt this was the best thing to do for my brothers to have a chance at living. So, she did what she thought was best for us.

As these 30 years have passed, I often think about Mick John. I wonder what he would've been like if he had a chance to grow up and become an adult. I'm sure he would've gone to play basketball in college. He wanted to go to Michigan State. He would've been a great husband and father. He loved going to church. He probably would've been a virtual member of my church.

The older I get, I've realized that grief never really goes away. It will always be here on Earth. But I'm so glad that I'm always learning and growing in how to deal with it in my way. With the help of the Lord, it is possible to move forward but not forget. Memories live on in our hearts. I love you, Thomas "Mick John" Weathersby.

The First One

Laurie Carrier

I became a physician to heal. I became a physician to tend to ailments, treat disease, and comfort in times of distress. I, like many of my colleagues, entered the field of medicine as an idealist. I wanted rewarding work which revolved around helping people live longer and healthier lives. I specifically chose the specialties of family medicine and psychiatry to carry out this plan. These two specialties kept me focused on preventative care and emotional well-being... or so I thought. I was focused on the outpatient setting, where I imagined all this utopic work would take place. Cancer screenings, physical exams, and other preventative healthcare was my jam. So, of course, when my first patient passed away unexpectedly, I was devastated... and confused.

I had seen Mr. Williams several times over three years as a family medicine resident and got to know him well. While working together, he cut down on smoking, lost 15 pounds, and was up-to-date with his cancer screenings. We both thought he was on the right track. So, I was crushed when his brother called me during clinic one day to let me know he had passed away peacefully at home. We had come so far together. How could this happen? Did I miss something... after all, I was a young physician, although I thought a comprehensive one. What did I do wrong? At that moment, I found his family comforting me. His brother let me know how meaningful our monthly check-ins were. Apparently, Mr. Williams would start getting ready a few days in advance and talk about it to anyone who would listen. He was always enthused by our conversations and new health goals set during our time together. What Mr. William's family was able to communicate was, in fact, I had done the job I signed up for. As I continued caring for my other patients, it didn't stop the tears and questions. I did enrich Mr. Williams's life just as he had enriched mine, teaching me valuable lessons that serve my patients and me today.

It took a few more years to understand that as outpatient physicians, we can guide, suggest, educate, and advise but, ultimately, we cannot choose the direction in which our patients' lives will go. We often just need to support them while they consider the help and guidance we offer. Ultimately, we can honor the autonomy of patients we are fortunate to encounter and can celebrate their stories, lives, and choices.

I was already out of residency when it struck me how our role goes beyond preventing, healing, and treating and extends into end-of-life choices. Helping somebody die with dignity and without pain or discomfort is essential to our work. With my double specialty, this often extends beyond terminal cancer into risky substance use or other life choices. Having raw and difficult conversations with high-risk patients and their families doesn't bring me joy. However, letting them know about my concerns and their risk of death due to overdose or the declination of necessary treatments is sometimes all I can do. Sharing information with love and compassion while not judging the decision is complex but essential. I am not up against the same collection of obstacles and life adversities that my patients are, and I need to respect their wishes, will, and journey. We see the problem and know the answer, but we do not have control over our patient's readiness to accept. I now see our role, not as lifesavers but as "life supporters." We support our patients where they are, and sometimes this role takes on the form of a life changer, a shoulder to cry on, a hand holder, a teacher, a friend, and support. Still, at the end of the day, we are their doctor, which is a unique role in itself.

A wise physician colleague, experiencing the loss of his daughter to breast cancer once told me "Happiness shared is happiness enhanced, and alas sorrow shared may diminish the sorrow." It is never easy to lose a patient, whether expected or not. And if none of the sorrow was acknowledged or shared, then a physician would experience a tremendous burden of grief over the years. Using opportunities to remember, share, learn from and educate others eases that pain and allows us to continue doing this wildly rewarding and wonderfully challenging doctor work. Thank you for allowing me to diminish some of that sorrow today.

No Regrets

As told by Yolanda Harris

I'm no stranger to grief and all the emotions that accompany it. I have had several relatives and friends die in my lifetime. All the relationships and circumstances were different. Some just saddened me, and others knocked the wind out of me. I had always found it most challenging when I was unclear about the state of their soul. I was raised knowing God is real. Therefore, so are heaven and hell. Though we don't know who makes it into heaven or hell, there is always a concern when people live a life outside God's will. There is nothing I can do about it now, but it makes my heart hurt. Grief where there is uncertainty hurts.

I remember the first time uncertainty took my breath away. It wasn't even because someone had died. Not in that moment anyway. I can't remember the exact words or why it even came up. I wasn't any older than nine when my cousin destroyed the world as I knew it. I remember going to my mother with this information. She was my mama—the only one I'd ever known. But she wasn't. Like many children, I was being raised by my grandmother but without my knowledge. That news changed me. Looking back, I believe that was my first experience with grief. I lost something. Even my grandmother said it. That information changed me.

Her love and affection still resonate with me today. It was never a question of her love for me or mine for her. I was crazy about her. Everything she did for me was appreciated. Even if it wasn't acknowledged at the moment. She taught me so much. I can't even begin to list them all. Sometimes I can hear her voice. "Always keep your house clean. You never know when someone is going to stop by." Sometimes I see her in my dreams. She doesn't say much, but her presence is there. She had a great impact on my life. When I lost her, there was peace for me. She'd expressed that she didn't want to die suffering, and she didn't. So, God allowed her to sleep away. I am grateful that God honored her request. I wasn't concerned about her soul. She was with the Lord.

Not only have I had challenges with a person's final destination being heaven or hell, but also how they transitioned. For example, when my grandmother died, she went peacefully. God also made sure her family didn't have to watch her suffer. But that's not the case for everyone. I remember when my aunt was murdered. She was in a city with no immediate family. I remember receiving the news, and all I could think was, "She's alone. She died alone. She's in a morgue alone." Sometimes I wonder what her last thoughts were. Did she call out for any of us? Did she call on Jesus?

I also had a cousin who was murdered. Like my aunt, he was alone in a city far from family. I remember when he made the decision to move. I didn't feel it was a good move for him, and I regret I didn't press a little harder about it. Even when you have a gut feeling about something, grown folks will do what grown folks want to do. So why waste your breath? Would it have been a waste though? Perhaps sharing and communicating with him more when he left could have changed the outcome. I wish I had encouraged him to maintain a relationship with God. Sometimes when we engage in activity in opposition to God's will for our lives, we allow that to disconnect us from Him. I get why that happens, but I have learned that it's not necessary. I wish I had reminded him to call on the name of Jesus in his time of trouble. Perhaps someone else did. My uncertainty bothers me.

My cousin's and aunt's deaths hit me hard because their lives were taken. Snatched. It's not that I love them more than anyone else that I've lost. They were robbed of their choice to live. I worry that they ran out of time and opportunity to secure their entry into heaven. Did my aunt have the opportunity to experience sobriety? Did my cousin have the opportunity to experience a life without anxiety and depression? He struggled with rejection. He didn't get to experience the love of being accepted by God. I have the opportunity to experience the very things I feel they missed out on.

I desire to go to heaven when I die. I pursue salvation daily to make that possible. I also want the same for my loved ones. Losing my aunt and cousin the way I did—with uncertainty—pushes me to engage in my remaining relationships differently. I am more intentional about sharing the Gospel. Not quoting scriptures to sound like a theologian but sharing the love and compassion that Jesus Christ instructs us to. Using every opportunity to be a light. Using every opportunity to introduce people to the Lord and encourage a relationship with Him. Perhaps that would even increase the quality of our earthly relationship. I don't get it right all the time. But the goal is to live with no regrets.

Redefining Grief

Katie Greer
Founder of the Satellite Project

Watermelon Wizz nail polish stared back at me in disappointment from the bathroom counter, its seal unbroken.

"She wanted me to paint her nails. I was going to … I just hadn't had time," I thought as my stomach churned.

Under the weight of emotional devastation, my body collapsed in the glass shower of the resort condominium. Hot water cascaded down my back to offer comfort, but I couldn't accept it. I tried scrubbing the sand out of my hair, screaming, but to no avail. Shame, anger, guilt, and regret berated whatever remained of my shell. How could my body carry her safely for nine months and then fail its sole duty nearly five years later? She was in my care, her hand held in mine when her life ended.

I felt trapped in a nightmare.

I failed my daughter.

I failed as her mother.

I failed.

In January 2016, we traveled with friends to Cabo San Lucas, bringing our eldest child. Marissa was so excited to swim in the pool and play with friends. Her thoughtful demeanor, intellect, and height made her appear two to three years older than her four years of age. When asked what she wanted to be when she grew up, without hesitation, she answered, "An Astronaut!" Marissa's affinity for the moon encouraged me to become more space-savvy. Earlier that day, she pointed to the blue sky, exclaiming, "Look, Mom, there's the moon!" She loved finding the moon and was usually successful, even in daylight. I held her, so proud of her awareness of her world. Unfortunately, two hours after this serene moment, my world shattered.

My friend, our kids, and I took in the view of the Pacific Ocean from the shore. Unfortunately, this highly sought-out vacation beach visit was my fatal mistake. A tall, strong wave loosened our footing, the second wave rolled in above our heads, and the current pulled us out to sea. We were rescued by two boats who shuttled us to the marina on the other side of the infamous El Arco.

Much of the details are blurry, but I recall the oxygen mask placed over my mouth in the ambulance while asking where my daughter was, waiting in a small exam room, begging to have someone come in to reassure me Marissa was alive. When the doctor opened the door, I cried and shivered in my ocean-soaked clothes.

"We were unsuccessful in reviving your daughter."

I pushed past him, running barefoot down the emergency department corridor to an open surgical room where my baby was lying intubated, lifeless, wearing only underwear.

I scooped her up. My mothering instincts believed she would breathe again if I tried. I aggressively swatted her back, hoping to hear a gasp.

My husband cried out, "What are you doing to her?"

I looked up with tearful despair, "Trying to get her to breathe!"

I rocked her limp body in my lap for hours.

Our group booked the next flight home. Law required us to leave her body in Mexico until a cargo plane could transport her home to the States. A heavy, protective level of shock settled into my core. Shock can be a scary place due to its unpredictability. I could not respond to questions or any stimuli. It felt like the world outside my body was pretending and moving slowly. Yet, I would occasionally get a sudden burst of reality and be flung forward into the present. It was in these moments that my outbursts occurred. Fits of rage.

I remember the dreadful airport interactions,

bewildering funeral service planning,

reporters knocking on the door to our home and calling us.

Safe boundaries were nonexistent. I read the horrific comments people posted about me online on social platforms. I remember these fragments of reality when the protective shock would shatter, and emotional outbursts were my only protection.

For weeks, crippling misery ran through my veins. I hated just about everyone, such disdain for those who got to keep their lives with their living children and seemingly joy-filled lives. I would mutter, "Don't get too acclimated to that. I used to be you." And the cherry on top? I was facing one of the ugliest words I had ever heard—grief. I held this word in such contempt. My lip curled at the offensiveness of its sound. Anytime someone used the G-word, I cringed.

As months passed, my ability to parent my youngest, now only, child was challenged with the question of whether I was equipped to be a mother. While searching for gifts one day, I came across a cheeky mug, the recipient being a young mom doing her best to get through the day with unruly toddler-aged children. It read: Kept the kids alive today! What humiliation. I read it and thought, "I could never own that ... well, I could, as a dark joke." I never purchased the mug. It was too dark, even for me. My negative self-talk had reached new lows, and what's a comforting companion when heading toward rock bottom? Alcohol. Most nights, I wished to not wake up the next morning.

Time pressed on, unphased.

Frequently drunk, I sat alone and cried. Being frustrated with friends, I cried harder. It seemed they had grown weary and tired of finding the right things to say. To not burn the years of friendship, I withdrew. Isolation was my new buddy. Sure, there were days when I laughed, went to coffee, finished a task at work, and some when I didn't cry, but nothing provided relief. I was in a mode of constant exhaustion. In 2018, I became increasingly aware as my son approached my daughter's age when she died. Soon after, he would embark on kindergarten, an adventure his big sister never had. This realization was excruciating. Sleepless nights paired with nightmares came flooding back with a vengeance. My memory was seared with events from that traumatic day. I felt continuously punished.

"I can't do this anymore!" So, that evening, I emailed a therapist asking for help.

Therapy nurtured love back into my soul, love that I had convinced myself I was no longer worthy of receiving. Months after psychological brain training, I regained self-awareness and relinquished the trauma from that day. Instead of deeply rooted anger and sadness, I was terribly sad, wishing I could time travel back to a year when life didn't ache. At this divergence I recalled a website bookmarked on my phone from 2016, The Grief Recovery Method (GRM), an evidence-based program with actionable steps for those seeking recovery in pain. "Wait, ewww, they used the G-word in the title." Aggravation aside, I acquired the purple paperback handbook.

I began reading and instantly knew this was what I needed. If a book could be a broken heart's soulmate, I had found it. This author articulated the emotions I was struggling through. The purple book felt like sunshine after years of fumbling through the darkness in a thunderstorm. I was so glad I found this. Tears fell from my eyes. Relief had arrived.

Simple but tough, I learned how to one, be honest about my emotions, all of them—even the ugly ones—and two, share my emotions. Nothing in life worth acquiring is simple, though. In fact, I'm certain the statement, "If it's too easy, you're probably doing it wrong," is on a shirt somewhere next to the bold mom mug. GRM wasn't easy, but it made my pain manageable.

Shortly after finishing the book, I enrolled in a GRM Specialist Certification course. Work granted me time off, and I carefully outlined the logistics to accomplish this milestone. Then, COVID-19 happened, and in-person events were discontinued. I feared class would be canceled, and my hope turned bleak. An email confirmation that the course would be virtual one week before the anticipated start date. The institute asked if I was still interested and available, and I gave a resounding affirmative.

Upon completion of the course, my grief narrative shifted, and I no longer desired to lessen my emotional intensity with the assistance of alcohol. My chest had been bound with anguish, holding on so tightly, aching to feel her presence. Grief is not only great sorrow but also the gift of experiencing greater joy; grief emotions are conflicting because human relationships are complex.

Today, my explanation of grief is diverse and is not limited to hope, sadness, memories, beauty, sorrow, lost dreams, joy, appreciation, respect, and immeasurable grace.

Last week, Watermelon Wizz caught my eye while perusing the nail polish aisle. First, I raised my hands and crossed them over my chest. Then, as I closed my eyes, I inhaled memories, a great longing, and the perpetual love I have for my little moon finder.

Really God

Shaleka Smith

On September 27, 2020, my baby, my nephew, laid down in the middle of the floor at his mother's house and died. I wasn't there, and I am sure there was more to it with the paramedics attempting to revive him, but in my heart, that is what happened. Dequan was the 27-year-old son of my late brother. Corral, Dequan's father, died in 1997 at 20. Dequan was his only son; everything about him was my brother, except his height. He had Corral's smile, laugh, and sense of humor. Dequan even had his father's appetite! I never saw anyone eat a burger like the two of them, meat patty first. He had diabetes like his father. When Dequan died, it felt like Corral died all over again. I was and still am devastated.

I remember my mom calling me in the middle of the night. She was hysterical. I'd never heard her like that before.

"I can't understand what you are saying." I knew someone must have died, but I thought it was her brother, who she was the caretaker of. I wasn't ready to understand what she was saying.

"My baby, he's gone." Even writing it now, my heart stops.

What do you mean gone?

He can't be gone.

I didn't have time to melt down. I had to get to my mom and then get to him. I knew that the 45-minute drive would be hard, and I needed to remain focused. So, I asked in my church's ministerial group chat that if anyone was up, to call me. One called and talked to me the whole ride to my mother's house.

We drove another 40 minutes to get to my nephew's mother's house. My mom, in true mom fashion, talked the whole ride. Why are you talking? Finally, I had to tell her I couldn't take her questions right now. At that point, I didn't know what I was walking into. I talked to my mom and his stepfather, and no one told me how he died. He was a young black man living in Chicago. Homicide crossed my mind, especially since that is how his father died. I didn't understand why we were going to her house. He didn't live with her. What was going on? I couldn't ask questions. Too many details would distract me. Just get there. It wasn't until I walked into his mother's house and saw him lying on her bedroom floor that I knew it wasn't foul play. But what happened? Later I learned he hadn't been feeling well that day. He'd started having trouble breathing. He never caught his breath; the paramedics couldn't revive him. He died right there in the middle of the floor. Since he died at home, the paramedics left him there, and the funeral home picked him up.

It was a long day; people were in and out of his mother's house all day. My mom didn't want to leave her until she fell asleep. We left, and I made the 45-minute drive to my mother's house, the 45-minute drive to pick up my daughter, and the 20-minute drive home. When I got home, I just needed to lay down. The only thing I'd said to God that day was, "Please get me to my destinations safely." When I got home, I could converse with my Heavenly Father. "Why didn't you warn me?" It sounds crazy that I'd expect God to warn me about somebody dying. It wouldn't have been a thought if he hadn't done it before. However, I remember having a dream before Dequan's father died. I was hanging out with my god-sister, and she disappeared, and we were never able to find her. Not long after that, my brother died. I remember having a dream before my father died and before my grandmother died. He'd warned me. Why didn't He this time? Not that God ever has to explain anything to me, but at that moment, I thought we were better than that. We were. His response was, "I did." Then I remembered the dream.

On September 17, 2020, I had a dream. A close friend of mine was preparing for her wedding. We were all around, helping her get dressed. Suddenly, she just stopped. She sat on the bed and refused to do anything else. We were all trying to understand her needs so we could help her on the most important day of her life. I remember saying, "Just tell me what you need. What can I do?" She kept saying she didn't want to do this anymore. She had a look that told me there was nothing we could do to change her mind. Finally, she laid down in the middle of the floor and died. When she took her last breath, I laid across her stomach and cried. I cried so hard in my dream that I woke myself up. I woke up weeping. It felt too real. I knew that wasn't just a dream. I did the only thing I knew to do next. I prayed. I remember the prayer verbatim, "Lord, I don't know who that was about, but I ask that they know you before they leave this earth." I'd gotten away from praying for things not to happen. Death isn't the worst thing that could happen. Dying and going to hell, now that is what scares me. So, I learned to pray for people's souls.

At first, I was grateful for the dream and for Him answering my prayer. Before my nephew said he couldn't breathe, he and his mother said the Lord's Prayer together. God was faithful. I thanked Him over and over. Until the Long Islands started to get to me. Then my gratitude turned into disappointment, frustration, and anger. Yup, I was angry at God.

Sir, why would you take my baby away?

You knew what this would do to us.

We are losing Corral all over again.

How could you do this to me?

It wasn't until I let Him get a word in that I could hear, "This wasn't personal."

I was taking it personally. After having such a hard time processing—and not processing—the death of Corral and my father, I couldn't understand why God would allow me to experience another devastating death. "Sir, you want me to die in my grief." When I think about it now, I realize I wasn't grieving according to 1 Thessalonians 4:13–14 (New Living Translation): "And now, dear brothers and sisters, we want you to know what will happen to the believers who have died so you will not grieve like people who have no hope. Since we believe that Jesus died and was raised to live again, we also believe that when Jesus returns, God will bring back the believers who have died with him." I had no hope. I couldn't see a way out of the sadness, the hurt, the disappointment, the anger. I wasn't remembering that God was faithful in my prayer request, ensuring I'd have the opportunity to see Dequan again in the Second Coming. That is not what you are thinking of when the pain is so intense you can't function, but after a while, the Holy Spirit will bring things back to your remembrance.

Temporarily Childless
Rachel Gaston-Porter

"I do!!"

This is the phrase I yelled out as I played dress-up with my younger cousin on Saturday afternoons.

As I grew—throughout high school and my young adult years—I daydreamed about the day I would stand at the altar looking my beau in the eyes as the preacher asked me to repeat after him. I mean, it's about every woman's desire to be someone's wife, right?

To have and to hold, for richer or poorer, sickness and health, until death do you part?

Hmph. Well, what if that death wasn't a literal one?

Grief is experienced in many forms. Death of a loved one, death of a child. But is grief acknowledged when a dream or desire dies? God has intentionally developed me to be who He designed me to be. However, the daily challenges of life had me breaking into pieces. Am I really supposed to cope with this?

For me, the answer was a hard "No." My "I do" became something I grieved passionately until I was on the verge of suicide.

How could my own body reject a gift so precious? I was shattered. Although I had a child before I met my husband, the thought of me birthing a starting lineup with my husband was something I looked forward to. Unfortunately, that season of my life brought forth a different seed. I later found out my stress levels were so high that my body went into fight mode and attacked the "foreign object" growing inside me.

The ideal marriage I put together was no longer important.

I couldn't have a child, my marriage was broken, and friends I thought I had, turned against me. I was rejected, ignored, broken, and clueless. Depression haunted me daily. I went to church sad and left church sad. People preyed on me to pray for me. As I grieved—sitting in the middle of my floor swaying back and forth, crying but making no sound, having a woe is me a moment—it hit me. It was as if a switch was aggressively flicked on. Everything flashed before my eyes, and I heard the voice of God say, "WHAT ARE YOU DOING? GET UP FROM THERE!! YOU KNOW WHAT YOU KNOW! HAVEN'T I ALWAYS BEEN YOUR ANCHOR? GET UP FROM THERE AND FIGHT!"

Honey! Those tears went from a "Why me" flow to an "It's me" command. I suddenly got angry. Angry at myself for losing sight of what this was. This was a spiritual attack. Satan had been out to destroy me and kill me since I was a little girl. Car accident, sickness, incarceration, and even a victim of assault. Now, this? Now through my marriage? How could I have been so blind?

Sis, listen! I got up with declarations and scriptures flowing out of my mouth.

"NO WEAPON FORMED AGAINST ME SHALL PROSPER"

"I AM THE HEAD AND NOT THE TAIL"

"I AM ABOVE AND NOT BENEATH"

"I AM MORE THAN A CONQUEROR THROUGH CHRIST JESUS"

"MY MARRIAGE IS CALLED ACCORDING TO YOUR PURPOSE GOD"

"GOD, I LOVE YOU, THEREFORE THIS WILL WORK OUT FOR MY GOOD"

These are just some things I began to declare that day! These, along with a few other scriptures and prayer partners, fasting, and believing have changed my life and marriage. Of course, we aren't perfect, but God has shown He is in control.

Scripture tells us to be angry but sin not. Anger showed up, but the Holy Spirit showed up, too! He came to comfort, heal, and deliver me from the enemy's trick. Sadly enough, I thought I was defeated. And because I thought it, I was. Oh, but when I came to myself! Hallelujah!! I was able to see God clearly. I am so grateful He helped me when I couldn't help myself. I just love God so much! And can I tell you, 7 months later, we were blessed with my 3-year-old. When he turned 2 years old, I birthed my daughter. And now, we also have another little boy. He brought me back to my "I do." God is faithful!

I pray this encourages someone to live, trust God, forgive and have the courage to believe again! Understand He loves you and will never forsake you! Satan is a liar, always has been, but that sucka is defeated, in Jesus' name!

My Son
Debra Allen

I stood at the bank of windows on the second floor of the
Evanston Civic Center that afforded a broad view of the main
entrance of the building where I worked and a large part of the
parking lot and surrounding neighborhood. The beautiful trees
and vast open area that was part of this city property were
quite beautiful. But today, the view was completely different
because I was watching my oldest child walk away from the
building and from me. Also, I remember it being rather
overcast. I don't know if it was because it was late in the day
or because of the darkness enveloping me.

I had never felt such pain. I felt like I was dying. Very slowly,
and very painfully, just slipping away. I couldn't seem to
catch my breath, and to be truthful, I wish I could have died
for just a few minutes. This was one of the moments in life
you dread, yet without moments like those, your children will
never really grow up.

I had been so hard on my son as he grew up because, as a
single mother, I wanted my little boy to grow up to be a man
... not just a male. I wanted him to be a responsible,
intelligent, hardworking, fun-loving, well-rounded,
trustworthy, confident young man who knew how to take care
of himself. And he was well on his way to becoming that
person. But to take the next step on his journey, he had to step
away from me and all that was familiar to him.

I had told him from when he was a very little boy that I would
take care of him until he was 18 and not a moment longer. He
never liked school, so that was not an option. Afterward, he
had to go to the service, find a job, move out, or be homeless!
But under no circumstances would I be taking care of him. I
was merely trying to get my bluff in early... I often wonder if

he knew that. I often wonder if he knows how much I love him.

Standing at the window that day was harder for me than bringing him into the world. When I held him for the first time, I couldn't consider him. ever leaving.

I reminded him to be careful and to make sure he let me know that he got there safely. I had to smile, wishing him well and not let him see that I was about to pass out from pain and anxiety. That was one of the hardest things I have ever done. I refused to let him see my heart breaking! After all, he was doing what I had told him to do—to live his life! I had told him that he could do anything he put his mind to and that he should be brave enough to live his dreams.

But the time had come, and the rubber was about to meet the road. He was leaving. He was moving away from home--not in the same city, not even the same state. No, my son was moving from Illinois to Colorado! Yep, you heard me…Colorado! Now I have made a concerted effort in sharing this story not to speak of race. Because a mother's love has nothing to do with race. But race has much to do with a mother's experiences, and unfortunately, in the country we live in, it does make a difference in how our children are treated. I was standing in the window watching my beautiful Black, firstborn, only son walk away from me into a world that I knew very well did not have his best interest at heart, and that is the very cleaned up, Christian version of what I was feeling at that moment.

I stood there, and my mind was bombarded with memories of my little boy. Bathing him and putting baby oil on his fat little body. I remember walking everywhere with him in tow. Recalling how my grandmother could never pronounce his name correctly, and she would call him "Rhyme." His name is Ryan! (I named him Ryan because I wanted him to be strong and kind like the cousin he was named for.) I stood there thinking of all the time I had spent trying to be the rough, tough Mom that I thought I had to be for him while praying that he never found out how many times I was hiding in the bathroom crying because all I really wanted to do was hold him. I had to be hard, strong, and insistent to prepare him for this moment. Wishing I had been a better mother to him. Wishing I had made fewer mistakes. Wishing I could have given him more, done more for him. Praying that what I had given him would be enough for him to survive and, against all the odds, thrive in this world that did not love my little boy and did not care about the man he had become.

Standing in that window, crying more than I did when my daddy died. Feeling a hurt that would change me forever, and finally realizing that this is all a part of being a parent. A parent has to love their child enough to let them go, enough to allow them to find their own path, enough to allow them to make their own mistakes, enough to always be there for them, but at a distance that is a comfort and not a crutch. This moment wasn't just about Ryan growing up. It was about Ryan growing me up too.

In The Prophet, Kahlil Gibran said, "You are the bows from which your children as living arrows are sent forth. The archer sees the mark upon the path of the infinite, and He bends you with His might that His arrows may go swift and far." It speaks to the fact that good parents must be strong enough to send our children far off into the world and the future. We must be strong enough to point them in the right direction, give them as much momentum as possible, and trust that God will take them where they were intended to land.

My son was 20 years old when he left home. It was two years after the 18-year mark I set, but the bluff did what it was intended to do. He has become an amazing man with many stories of his own to tell and some that I am sure he never will! I would love to hear his version of this same event. When we listen to our children's viewpoints of events, they are very rarely the same as ours. I am so grateful that Ryan gave me one of the greatest titles I will ever carry: Mother. I am so proud of him, the amazing person that he is. He is an incredible father, and I am grateful he is My Son.

Special Delivery

Mellisa Michael

I had dreamt of how my pregnancy would be. I was filled with excitement when I found out my time had come. Pregnancy and childbirth are beautiful experiences, and I would enjoy every minute of them. During my pregnancy, I was healthy and glowing. I was excited to meet my son.

There are some details of my labor and delivery that I do not remember. It was a complex situation that escalated really quick. I expressed some concerns during my last prenatal appointment before my due date. I was uncomfortable. My legs, feet, and hands were swollen to the point that I couldn't do anything. Since this was my first pregnancy, there were things that I assumed were expected but were still concerning. My doctor assured me that I was experiencing "normal pregnancy symptoms" and that "things would pass." My anxiety was eased. Who doesn't trust their doctor's words? A few nights later, I wished I had trusted my gut more.

I was lying in bed, trying to get some sleep. Then, out of nowhere, I felt a strong thump in my stomach. I jumped out of bed immediately and ran to my then husband. I thought I was in labor. We called and spoke with the on-call doctor. Her advice was to go to the hospital. I was stuck between being excited about meeting my son and scared that something was wrong. I kept thinking about the conversation in the doctor's office a few days earlier. When we arrived at the hospital, they began to run some tests. We learned that I had developed preeclampsia, which impacted my kidney function. My labor was induced, and after 24 hours, my son was born. I was happy. Now everything would be okay.

I was excited about breastfeeding. I was blessed to enjoy that bonding experience for a week. However, after a week, the doctors shared that I had an infection and could no longer breastfeed. I was devastated. My whole womanhood was being stripped away. It is ideal for a woman to be able to breastfeed her baby. Now all I had was holding him and gazing into his beautiful eyes. I was thankful to have a healthy baby boy.

I was still swollen and could barely walk to the bathroom. During my delivery, my vaginal area was severely torn and required stitches. One morning I went to the bathroom and noticed excessive bleeding. I called for the nurse, and after assessing the situation, she called for the doctor. Before long, I was rushed into emergency surgery to stop the bleeding. The loss of so much blood required a blood transfusion. This was the first of many.

Things began to go downhill from there. I started to have trouble breathing. They tried putting me on oxygen, but I refused because I was okay. I wanted to be okay. After running more tests and scans due to my breathing, they found blood clots in my lungs. I was immediately put on a blood thinner. My health continued to decline. Two weeks after my son was born, I was transferred to ICU and was put on a ventilator. My family shared with me that my heart stopped at one point. For most of my time in the ICU, I was sedated. After being taken off the ventilator, I understood what was happening. I was confused about why I was still in the hospital. I just wanted my son. He was my motivation, as I had a long road ahead.

I'd lost my ability to walk and had to regain my strength. I had to endure extensive physical therapy. I was confused and frustrated because I wanted a healthy delivery and to go home with my newborn. Two months in the hospital was not part of my plan. I remember telling God, "You did this to me," "I did not deserve to almost lose my life." My faith in God was lost as the time in the hospital passed. I was depressed and away from my son for two months. I missed sweet precious moments with him. It still affects me to this day. I am still healing and overcoming a few things from the pregnancy. However, I can look back and give God the Glory. It's a blessing to be able to TELL my testimony.

My depression continued to deepen; I wanted to die. I couldn't understand why this happened to me. I felt that God was punishing me for some reason. The guilt I experienced pushed me to the point of giving up. Why couldn't I have had a typical experience? Why was I lying in a hospital bed connected to a thousand monitors? My family, church family, and friends came to visit me every day, and I cried every time someone left. I hated being confined to the hospital bed. I felt like I was no longer connected to the outside world.

My two-month stay at the hospital moved me through each hospital unit as I progressed. After completing extensive inpatient rehab for two weeks, I was finally discharged from the hospital. I was going to be reunited with my son. I was set up with home health for physical therapy. I had no idea that the actual recovery phase was beginning. The physical therapist came to my home three times a week. I was on several medications. There was definitely progress, but I was still physically weak.

I needed more support with my daily needs. It was hard to accept that, and I was frustrated. Not only could I not take care of myself, but I couldn't take care of my son independently. It was a significant adjustment to get back to me and learn motherhood. I hated having to learn to take care of myself all over again. There were many moments when I didn't feel like I deserved to be a mother. My son was well taken care of by his godparents, especially when I was in the hospital. But I, his mother, who carried him in my womb, knew nothing about him. I was helpless, hopeless, and angry all the time.

The postpartum depression made things challenging. I never told anyone that I was struggling. I never told anyone that I had thoughts of ending my life. I figured that this whole experience was more than stressful for my family. I was guilty of even going through it all. Although I didn't lose anyone, I still experienced grief.

I lost a piece of myself.

I lost time.

I lost moments with my newborn son.

I blamed God and myself. I would spend hours just crying. Demanding to see my son. I wanted to give up. But I couldn't. As much as I hated that I missed the first two months of my life, I knew I couldn't miss the rest of his life.

I pushed through.

Each time I saw my son, I pushed.

I had to fight for my life; I pushed.

I knew that if I continued pushing to get to a better place, the bond I wanted with my son would come. The more I tried, the more I gained strength. Physical strength and spiritual power. As time went on, my faith in God was restored and strengthened. I know He is accurate and has my best interest at heart. Sometimes God allows us to go through things to bring us closer to Him. Even when you can't understand the reason or purpose. I declared that God is my healer, and He did just that.

My experience gave me a passion for working with pregnant women. Suppose anyone ever goes through something similar to this. In that case, I want them to know even when it seems impossible to overcome, the Word of God says there is a promise in our lives. We must remember that the Lord will never put more onus than we can handle. The lowest places in our life produce the most perseverance.

Gardner

As told by Ikari Gardner Sr.

I never stopped needing my father, and I don't think any boy
or man ever does. We just learn to navigate life without a
father because we never had one or lost ours to different
circumstances. For me, it was death. It has been many years,
and there hasn't been one moment that I didn't wish he was
here. My father was my best friend - my imperfect best friend.
He was always honest with me about his personal flaws, but it
never took away from our relationship. I was closer to him
than my mom, who I lived with. That's how it needed to be.

I was one of the few boys in my neighborhood with a father. I
am grateful that even when my parents separated, they were
mature enough to co-parent. My father was always there
supporting everything I did. He nurtured my baseball team for
other young boys and me in the neighborhood. I never had an
issue sharing my father with my friends because he had
enough love for us. He celebrated us all! He was there for it
all, big or small wins, taking us to eat after practice and
games. He was present, not just around. Every day after work,
he would come home, and we would go to the park and
practice. Whether he had a good day or a bad one. I appreciate
that so much more as an adult because I see the effects on
young men that don't have a strong male presence growing
up. I still had youthful challenges, but my father would only
let things go so far.

He always called me "Gardner." He never called me by my
first name. Whenever he had extra bass in his voice, I knew he
meant business. That wasn't very often. He didn't need to yell
at me to get my attention. We always had open conversations,
and he always held my attention. I value the conversations we
had because many of them I have had with my own sons.
There weren't many lessons I had to learn from the streets

because my father would talk me through things. He never tried to scare me straight. He gave me all the facts so I would make good decisions in life. I never feared letting him down because that wasn't a possibility. He was one of the most laid-back people I knew. He had his own life hiccups, so he wasn't in the business of condemning people when they had challenges.

I always thought it was bizarre that my dad went through his rebellious stage later in life. However, I later learned it made sense because he had a sheltered childhood. He went after the things he hadn't experienced as a teenager and young adult in his forties and fifties. After his passing, I talked with my mom about why she put him out when I was a child. She explained that he'd started drinking and doing drugs, interfering with his home responsibilities. I can't say I remember anything different with him during those times. All my memories are positive. I wonder what attracted him to drugs. I am sure he saw plenty of people struggle with addiction before he got hooked.

I know he would still be here if drugs hadn't gotten ahold of him, though it wasn't just the drugs he was addicted to. He'd developed this attraction to younger women. He was getting older, and his girlfriends were getting younger. That ended up being more of a problem as time went on. He just wanted to experience what he'd missed in his youth. We don't always consider the importance of certain life experiences and what missing out on them can do to some people. Whenever I questioned his life choices, he would say, "Man, I'm just out here having fun." His fun ended up being our heartbreak. He didn't see how his decisions were affecting his family. Both his parents had to watch him struggle. The drugs weren't the cause of his death, but the damage was already done. Years before he died, he went to rehab and was clean. I had my dad back for a while.

My dad never wanted to worry me about things. So, I was the last to know when he was diagnosed with cancer. By the time I found out, his cancer was at stage 3. I knew something was wrong because he was losing weight fast. Even now, I get concerned when I see people lose weight at an accelerated rate. He still worked. He worked until he was bedridden. Once I learned of his condition, I didn't want to leave his side. I didn't want him to go through things by himself. The more time I spent with him, the more I learned about things he'd kept from me. I knew he didn't have much time left. I spent time trying to get his affairs in order. He warned me of the challenges I would have with certain family members. It wasn't long before I understood what he was referring to.

I couldn't focus on anything but the fact that my dad was dying. My dad's sister wasn't making it easy, but the things she was after I didn't need. She was focused on the money. I was so angry. My father was worth more to me than a few thousand dollars. She could have everything if it meant keeping my dad. But, it wasn't that simple. Every day I watched him lose strength. Every day I watched him losing his life. Every day was a reality that he would no longer be around one day soon. I didn't have time for my aunt and her foolishness. All I had time for was ensuring my dad was comfortable and cared for. Anything outside of that was a blur.

Most things after he died were a blur. I'd lost my best friend. I didn't know life without him, which was hard to process. Finally, I had my head together enough to make his funeral arrangements. Following that, I spent every day hurt. Days turned into weeks and weeks into months. There are no words that can really describe my hurt. How do you describe when your go-to person is gone? His advice is gone. His jokes are gone. His presence is gone. No one can prepare you for that. I knew it was coming, and I wasn't prepared. I needed my dad and still do.

I will never get my dad back. I was blessed with brotherly support from some men a few years later. I didn't realize how much I needed it. I'd gotten married since my father's death and gotten closer to my mother. Yet I needed that male connection. There are things I just can't talk to my ladies about. God knew what I needed. He also sent me a spiritual father that really looked out for me. Things about marriage that I didn't get to learn from my biological father, I learned from my spiritual father. His advice was sound like my dad's. I trusted him. He has also passed away. That is recent, and it's been hard. I've lost both my dads, but they made me a better man. I think my dad would be proud of the man I have become.

I Need My Mom

Shaun Carr

"Moms in heaven now," are not the words anyone wants to hear. Those four words changed my life on April 16, 1993. I was 15, and my brother gave me the worst news in the world. My initial reaction was sadness mixed with shock. How? I don't understand. I prayed that she would get better. Heaven? I knew she was having health issues, but heaven? No one told me she was terminally ill and would die. She didn't tell me she was that sick. Why didn't she tell me? There were so many questions. Some that were later answered and others that may never be.

Many memories are faded because I was so young when my mother died. I depend on my brother, who is 12 years older than me, to jog my memory. I do remember how loving and firm she was. There wasn't a time when she didn't put my brother and me first. Education was important to her. She made sure we went to good schools. I went to Christian and Catholic schools, as religion was just as important. She had an empathetic nature. I believe it came from the work that she did. My mom was a social worker with the Department of Children and Family Services. She did this work until a year before she died.

I guess I didn't understand how sick she was because she continued to live what I thought was her normal life. In early 1988 she was diagnosed with breast cancer. She went through chemotherapy, had a mastectomy, and went into remission. Things were hopeful, but in 1989 cancer returned. She seemed to be doing well, but in 1991 there was a domestic dispute between her and my father. It was traumatic for all of us. I can hardly even talk about it to this day because I feel like it led to my mother getting sick again. At that point, cancer metastasized. The stress made things worse.

My mother began to make frequent visits to the hospital. I knew she was sick, but I didn't know she was dying. Probably in my adolescent mind, mothers didn't die. She was such a strong person. I thought she was getting better. More importantly, I prayed that she would get better. My mom made sure we had strong faith. We had a faith-based home. I believed wholeheartedly that when I asked God for something it would happen. I believed that my mom would be healed by my prayer. The fact that she wasn't, left a strain on my relationship with God. I trusted that prayer worked, and it didn't. I've lived in that place for a long time. "Prayer changes things," seems more like a tagline than truth.

Over the years, I've struggled to reconcile a belief in God with a lack of belief in prayer. I believe that God exists, but I no longer believe prayer changes the outcome of anything. For example, had I been told that my mom would die, I would have been devastated, hurt, and perhaps angry. But I also believe my faith at the time would have helped carry me through. Instead, her death came as a slap, and I've never gotten over that. For the past 29 years, my grief over her death has manifested itself differently, from my lack of religious faith to my self-destructive tendencies. I have been mad at the world more or less since that fateful day.

I am disappointed in God, but I am way more disappointed with my mom. Why wouldn't she have a conversation with me about her health? I wasn't an adult like my brother, but I wasn't a child. I was at the age of understanding. It would have been nice to be warned. I believe that they didn't want to devastate me. However, it ended up happening anyway. Maybe if they had told me, I would have understood better when she died. Even when she went to the hospital, I would always think they would help her, and she would return. As I think about it, maybe I knew but not hearing it from her mouth didn't make it real.

It got to the point where she couldn't be home alone because she started to have accidents. I remember her falling a lot. She is the only person I've ever seen in life deteriorate from cancer. It was odd to see because she was the queen of the house. Without really having anyone at home to take care of her, it was decided she would move in with my grandmother. At one point, a DNF (Do Not Feed) order was discussed. That confused me. I asked my brother what would happen if she didn't eat. His response was, "Then it will be you and me."

It was just that—my brother and me—once my mother died. My brother became my legal guardian. It was rough. At 27 he instantly had these responsibilities that he didn't create himself. I appreciate that today because he didn't hesitate. He now had a mortgage, bills, an angry teenager, and grief. He was stressed. We were constantly at each other's throats. I don't think we were angry with one another, but we were both angry and hurt and didn't know how to process what was happening. I appreciate him taking on that responsibility because he didn't have to. I needed to keep some stability in my life. As inexperienced as he was in being a guardian, he did a good job. I think my mother would be proud.

I don't think she would be as pleased with me. Seeing my mother's health decline should lead me to better care for myself. Even after having health scares, it seems hard for me to do. I wish I could apologize for my neglected health. I would also apologize for my inability to maintain the religious conviction she instilled in me as a child. I would tell her that I was still not over her death. After 29 years, I'm not over it. I don't visit her grave. I don't want to hear about people's plans for Mother's Day. I thought I'd be in a place of celebration by now, but I'm not. In some ways, I am still that 15-year-old boy not understanding how my mother is in heaven. When she should be here with me.

One Day at A Time

Jamie Ellingwood

I think it's common for people to misremember loved ones
when they die, especially after a certain amount of time
passes. Maybe we all put on some rose-hued glasses to protect
the person's memories and ourselves, but all I remember is
love. It's been 14 years since my dad died. Some days it feels
like yesterday. What my dad is, was, and continues to be to
me, is someone who seemed to have an unlimited amount of
time and energy to give to the things he loved and gave him
purpose. I remember him once saying, "I don't get bored."
When he died, we said he had packed twice as many years
into his short life of only 51. He was someone who worked
hard and received accolades at his day job, then attended to
the gritty work of painting and rehabilitating rental properties
many evenings, yet somehow always made time for the
family. I don't remember a school concert, art fair, or event he
didn't attend. I have many memories of biking to get ice cream
or playing football in the backyard. If there was one thing he
wasn't good at, it was patience and slowing down. Even on
vacation, he had trouble just lying around and relaxing. If he
had to sit still and "relax," he'd still be listening to a book on
tape.

His health was the most striking thing, which made his death
so shocking. He'd always been active and consistently made
time to play basketball, tennis, and golf multiple times a week.
His boss made fun of him for being the only guy his age who
could wear out the soles of gym shoes like a kid.

Dad was someone that held himself to high standards and
pushed himself to always do better. We used to go to his
basketball games, and while he would say "Let's go" to the
team, he was mostly heard pushing himself—"Come on,

Bill!"—when he'd miss a layup or free throw. He was a man bent on self-improvement. We joked that New Year's Day was his favorite holiday because he loved resolutions and encouraged us to make them. One year he got out a whiteboard on January 1 and propped it in front of the family to help us draft them.

Above all else, he wanted the best for us. That was evident in everything he did. His father was a factory worker, and my dad was one of eight kids. He saw the differences in job and life opportunities afforded to him compared to his siblings, who hadn't attended college. So, for his kids, a college education was not an option but an expectation and something discussed frequently. He was a planner and consistently worked to give us opportunities he knew would put us ahead in the world. We were routinely asked to participate in filling out checks and bills at the kitchen table and expected to mow the lawn and complete chores. He was intent on educating us on personal budgets and finances. To a willing audience, he strived to ensure we knew how privileged and fortunate we were. Having a stable, supportive father is a privilege and fortune, but to have one so committed to our wellbeing and success was, and continues to be, an enormous gift.

The irony of my dad's death is that as I left for my trip, he was concerned that I was going across the world by myself and was worried for my safety.

I had been in Zambia for about a week on a PA school clinical rotation doing HIV research. It was a Sunday in August, and Dad was out playing golf with some friends. He went to tee off, but he didn't have his clubs. He seemed a bit confused, and his friends thought it was odd, but they continued to play out the remainder of the holes. After the game, his friend drove him home. He took a nap, but when he woke up, he couldn't see out of one eye, and my mom rushed him to the ER. His first CT scan was fine, and they were ready to release him. However, they did a second scan for good measure and realized he'd had a massive stroke.

I was notified of the stroke after a day or two due to technology and time changes across the globe. For a few days, he seemed to be doing well. My friends went to visit him in the hospital. He had conversations with colleagues, and my grandparents drove in from out of town. At one point, he tried to get his shoes on to leave! I was able to call and tell him I loved him but didn't make plans to head home since the hospital staff was talking about him going to rehab and coming home. I figured my mom would need the most help when he was at home.

But, while all this was happening, Dad's brain was swelling. And it kept swelling. He compensated for a long time until he couldn't any longer, and they had to AirCare him to another hospital for emergency surgery. The surgery would involve removing half of his skull to allow the brain to swell outward and limit the pressure on the healthy side of his brain and the parts of his brain that affect baseline functioning like breathing. I got on the first flight home. I was halfway around the world, and it was the longest journey you can imagine. I tried to watch lighthearted kids' movies on the plane back to the US to pass the time, and they just made me cry. Sitting for 17 hours with just your thoughts, hoping that you can see your dad before he dies, is excruciating.

I landed in DC and called my mom. He was getting worse. I was now, at least in the US, but still so far away. I called my friends and asked for thoughts, prayers, miracles, and all the positive vibes they could possibly muster to add to the universe to keep him going. When I arrived home, my friends picked me up from the airport and drove me directly to the hospital. It was like a wake. My grandparents, uncle, mom, brother, and sister all stood in the ICU room. He was there. He was alive but unconscious and had no idea I was there. The

115

pity in the room was palpable. The ICU staff always knows the truth. They have seen this before. They know stats and vitals, what is stable, what is "good," and what is declining. They had been bolusing him full of salt water, trying to get the swelling to shift out of his brain, but his body resisted. His brain had been insulted so deeply that no surgery or saline could take down the inflammation. All the salt water started to cause his kidneys to shut down. His brain continued to swell. It pushed on his healthy brain tissue. It pushed down toward the brain stem. Less than a day after I returned home, his condition worsened. The doctors confirmed his condition was permanent and wouldn't improve. It had been 6 days since he was out enjoying a Sunday game of golf with his friends. We made a choice to take him off life support. He took his last breaths, surrounded by the family that loved him beyond words.

Then, everything was a rush. I remember being mad and sad. Upset and disbelieving. His death was unexpected, so there was a lot of going through the motions just to do the things needed because you're supposed to do them. Going to pick out a casket, deciding on what type of service and what songs to sing and who and what readings were to be done. Things seemed so stupid and pointless. The family was coming into town. There were people all over the house. I just wanted them to go away. Then, things like death certificates, lawyers, paperwork, and files. There was a huge hole, but also this huge mass of other stuff that was wedging its way in, trying to fill that void. It was all just a blur.

His friends and colleagues found themselves investigating their own mortality. We heard stories of colleagues having near-death experiences, and Dad was there with them. Others who had learned to better recognize the signs of a stroke. Others getting preventative and screening tests to know their risk status. "If this could happen to Bill, this could happen to me."

I spent nights sleeping in bed with my mom. We were all in shock and dismayed that this could possibly be real. I had trouble sleeping. I gritted my teeth and tightened my fists. Eventually, I started taking medication and seeing a counselor.

I finished PA school, broke up with my serious boyfriend, and moved by myself to a small rural town in the mountains of North Carolina. I was starting a new career as a PA, but more importantly, I was starting the healing process. My work schedule allowed me to go hiking one or two times a week, and I found my healing in the trees and mountains. I found it in the crunch of dirt under each step and concentrating on my breath—inhaling and exhaling. I'd talk to my dad, talk to God, listen to the birds, I processed. I was lucky to have this time and space. I found space to be the most important of healing mechanisms. It allowed for a conscientious unpacking. It's like taking off big, leaden football shoulder pads. They are so heavy. And you're taking them off ounce by ounce.

I learned that grief is a journey. There were many days when I could distract myself, and some days I couldn't. There were also days when grief would surprise me, and seemingly out of nowhere, I'd be sad and tearful. Fourteen years later, there are still days when grief surprises me. But, there were also many times when memories would catch me midday and make me smile. I'd see his favorite candy in the store, or his favorite sports team would be in the news. Some people who haven't experienced close grief may think they should avoid talking about the deceased because it will just make the person grieving feel sad. The best healing came from openly talking about my dad with friends and family. Telling a story or sharing a memory. It kept him alive and still does. I wish he were here to share my successes, moves, job, and life changes. There are innumerable times I've wanted to call him or ask him a question or lean on him for advice or have him help me in ways my friends' fathers help them, but he's just not physically here. It seems to me that out of grief comes a natural resilience. As the bereaved, you have no choice but to keep living life. Something you thought you could never get through, you somehow do. There is strength in that. My dad's favorite line was, "How do you eat an elephant? One bite at a time." When I thought I couldn't get through the grieving process, the only choice was to take one bite at a time. To wake up, get out of bed, and start a new day.

Senior

Anonymous

I've never talked about it. No one ever asked me how I felt about it. Nor have I been eager to talk about it. Neither my feelings nor my opinion were considered when decisions were made. I've lived with this traumatic life experience for the past 22 years. It's probably not healthy, but it wasn't about me. It was about taking care of the people my father left me with: my mom, my older sister, and my younger brother. I was 19, and I'd instantly become the man of the house. Not because I'd earned this role. Not because I decided to start a family. Not because I was the best candidate for the job. I was now the man of the house because my father, Senior, had died. I was barely legal. I still needed the guidance and wisdom of my father. There was no way I could fill his shoes.

My father passed away from sarcoidosis of the lungs. This inflammatory disease progressed quickly, causing his lungs to deteriorate. We heard the words families hate a doctor to say; there was nothing else they could do. Senior was dying. My brain couldn't process what was happening. This was my dad. My friend. My guide through life. I was struggling to figure life out before he got sick. Now how was I going to find my way? Who was going to give me advice? Who was going to encourage me not to settle into labels? Where would I get my fatherly love from?

I had a front-row seat to my father's health declining. I spent much time with my mom as she navigated the healthcare system. There were a lot of doctor's offices and hospital visits. Though I had the stature of a man, I was still a boy, and it was a lot to digest. I had to be there for my mom, so there wasn't much emotion I could express. I just sat and listened and observed. Some discussions went over my head, but there was a theme. My dad wasn't going to get better. Once that was established, there was a shift.

Relatives traveled to be with our family during this time. I had never met most of these people. They were never around while I was growing up.

Why were they here?

Why are they giving their opinion?

Who invited them?

I was angry. My father raised his family alone, separate from all these long-lost relatives.

Why was it important for them to be here while he was dying?

Why weren't they around while he was in the condition to make memories?

While he could talk and laugh with them.

While he could break bread with them. Senior's better days were behind him.

What kind of people come around when someone is dying? I struggled for many years with the instant family that came when Senior's health was failing. I understand now that we needed support. Especially my mom. She had to make the hardest decision most people ever make. Senior was being taken off the ventilator. There was a tiny chance that he could breathe on his own. She was about to lose her life partner. Her best friend. Her love. Her co-parent. She had people around, but Senior's death would create a void for all of us.

We needed him.

I needed him.

He wasn't done raising me.

Senior was a better man than I could ever be. He put forth much effort to be a good person and treat people right. He had the same expectation for us. All his life lessons are embedded in my heart and mind. He kept me close. I was his namesake and oldest son. I idolized him. Whatever he said was golden. If he told me I could go to the moon, I believed it. If he had an idea to do something, he did whatever it took to get it done. Since I was always around him, I saw him turn nothing into something often. He worked with his hands. Most of the time, he was fixing cars. I get my passion for cars from him. He reassured me in knowing we could start and finish anything. Results are dependent on the work you put into something. I saw him work hard, and he always produced results.

Senior started teaching me at a very young age about cars. He would explain things so I could understand, and I learned quickly. It reached a point where I could complete tasks without him. He trusted in my abilities and what he'd taught me. It was exciting for several reasons. Senior gave me the first opportunity to make my own money. "Give your brother some money for his pocket," Senior said. My confusion and annoyance must have been apparent. "I want you to show him what it's like to have money in his pocket." Though I would have never done this on my own, I understood. Senior wanted me to care for my brother, just as he'd taken care of me. I saw my father often look out for the people he loved. I try my best to mirror that behavior.

I always saw Senior as a strong person. Even until his death. If a dying man could be strong, I had to be. Or at least seem to be strong. They needed me. I had to push my feelings aside and be whatever my family needed me to be. Senior was the template, but now I needed to make this role my own. Truth is, we needed Senior. Without him, we were all lost. We all were weighed down with hurt. I'd say we were processing, but what does that even mean. I don't think I ever processed Senior's death. I spent so much time trying to fill everyone else's void that my own got bigger.

No one can tell you how lousy grief feels. It's an indescribable pain. Even if someone warned me, I wouldn't have understood. I had nineteen years with my dad, and it wasn't enough.

"Why didn't I spend more time with him?"

The guilt I was feeling tormented me. I didn't have anyone to talk to. Would that have helped? I was feeling so many things, and I don't know if I would have been able to express them. I didn't depend on God because my anger had developed into spiritual hate. Before Senior died, I was trying to be intentional about knowing God. Senior's death changed that. I had nothing to say to God. I carried that anger for so long that I didn't know how to ask for help. I needed to talk to someone. I needed internal healing.

As time went on, I adapted to this new life without Senior. Since I no longer had him to create memories, I sought out his siblings. They'd known him longer than I did, and they would have childhood stories to share. In sitting among my uncles, I not only learned more about Senior, but I also developed my own relationships. When Senior was alive, I didn't know these men. Yet, in his absence, I grew close to them. In many ways, Senior passed the baton to them. I miss Senior. No one could take his place. Yet, I appreciate them stepping in to be what he could no longer be.

Grandma Mena

As told by Nicole Henry

I haven't had many experiences of loss in my life. I am grateful for that. However, the loss I experienced hurt me more than I realized. Preparing to participate in this book, I realize how much I miss my granny. Grandma Mena was my paternal grandmother. She left an imprint on my life that has become visible to me over the years, especially since I have become a mother. Grandma Mena was such a nurturer. How she cared for me as a child will always stick in my memory. I wish I had spent more time with her as I got older. I didn't realize I wouldn't have her around forever.

I saw her take her last breath. I wasn't aware of what was happening at the moment. It was the first time in my life that I'd seen someone die.

She had spent a week or two in the hospital. She'd been battling breast cancer and having some challenges with her diabetes. She had a stroke during the night, and the doctors determined that there was nothing they could do. It was hard to believe because she was alert the day before. After her stroke, she was awake and could hear us, but she wasn't talking. They advised our family to transition her to hospice, and we agreed.

Knowing she didn't have much time, our family gathered at the hospital. There were so many of us. There were 15 or 20 people in the room and flowing into the hall. We all just wanted to be there. Maybe we thought she wouldn't want to leave if she felt all the love. At that moment, I wished I'd taken advantage of spending time with her more as I got older. At that point, whatever time she had, I just wanted to be there. I've often heard that people will hold on before transitioning to see a particular person. For Grandma Mena, it was Cousin Larry.

People knew she was waiting for Cousin Larry. Cousin Larry was one of her favorite people. We let her know when we knew he'd made it to the hospital. People were saying, "Larry is here, Larry is here." I can still see her take a faint breath and open her eyes wide. I was standing next to the hospital bed, and immediately I had high hopes. I said, "Look, Uncle Joe, she's awake." It wasn't what I thought. It was the opposite. My grandma was taking her last breath. Though we'd been with her for hours, waiting for that moment, I wasn't ready. I couldn't even be in the room anymore.

There was more emotion in the room than I could handle. I usually process emotions privately. Not many people have seen me cry. At that time, I don't know if any of my family members had ever witnessed me be emotional. I just became quiet. The first thing that came to mind was to call my sister, who was away at college, to tell her Grandma Mena had passed. It hit me once I said, "She's gone." I wailed, something I'd never done in front of people. I couldn't control my emotions, just as I couldn't control Grandma Mena leaving. I would never get to spend another moment with her.

Though I was not my father's only child, I don't remember sharing Grandma Mena with anyone else. When I visited her on weekends, it was always just her and me. I had siblings and cousins; I don't remember them being there. All her attention was on me. She was so attentive and kind. I loved being around her. The only time I remember her doing anything resembling fussing was when she gave me water at night and then warned me not to wet the bed. I remember sleeping with her and watching her evening ritual. She would straighten up around the house. She would end her routine by putting rollers in her hair.

I don't know which beauty was more radiant, her inward or outward beauty. She would get dolled up every day. She would wear her hair straight with it slightly curled on the ends. Her jet-black hair was everything! You would never catch her with her hair slipping. I was the only one she would let play in it. She would always wear red lipstick when going out. I believe it made her feel more like a lady. She was always put together, even lounging around the house. I don't remember her going further than the porch, but if she had to go anywhere, she was ready. I remember spending many summer days on the porch watching the kids get out of high school. Playing with her magnifying glass. Swatting flies. Eating hot dogs and burgers.

She was intentional about how she looked. She was intentional about how she treated people as well. Her loving and caring presence is what I believe drew people to her. I enjoyed all the time we spent together, and I don't have any bad memories. However, I wish we would have made more memories before she died.

When I became a teenager, spending time with my grandmother wasn't a priority. I was interested in my friends. When someone has been in your life your whole life, there is no concept of them not being there. I never pictured not being able to visit her when I wanted and get some good breakfast! Grits, sausage, bacon, and toast with grape jelly on the side. She always had the grape jelly next to the grits, which would get mixed together, and to this day, I eat grape jelly with my grits. I thought she would be around for every milestone in my life. If I had spent more time with her, I might have known who she was outside of my grandmother. There was so much more to her. She worked, I believe, for 45 years at the same place. I didn't get to hear her stories about work. I didn't get to hear stories about how she grew up or hear her tell me what my father was like as a child. I lost the opportunity for all that. Since her death, I've relied on stories from family.

Even though I don't talk about her much, she impacted my life. When I had my daughter, I wished she could have had the same experiences with Grandma Mena. Unfortunately, that wasn't possible, but I am intentional about creating similar memories. For example, my passion for cooking could be credited to Grandma Mena, and I try to have my daughter in the kitchen as much as possible while cooking. I want to give her as much of Grandma Mena as I can. I remember asking my daughter if she had met Grandma Mena when she was in heaven. I don't know if heaven even works that way, but I hope they crossed paths. I am blessed to have had my Grandma Mena. Though I wish we had more time, our time is cherished.

Dealing With It

Felicia Warner

Losing a mother, sister, brother, father, niece, nephew, grandparent, or anyone close to you is never easy. It's like getting hit when you never expected it or having the rug swept from under you. No one ever teaches you how to live without them or talks about how to live when someone you love has made their transition. Loss is never the same. Often it is so painful that you don't want to go on, but YOU MUST.

As kids, we plan our entire life out—finish school, get married, have children, buy a big house, and get a great job. Well, you get my point. You don't think twice about how in a moment, you could lose the rock, comedian, and the go-getter of the family; then just like that, you must face that truth.

My story begins with my first actual experience of losing my beautiful, loving, God-fearing, and compassionate niece. My niece battled the complications of lupus for 13 years and never complained. I watched her lose limbs. Felt like she was losing her mind, but then she would bounce back. However, this horrible disease had taken its toll on her. She started to lose hope. I did too, but I never shared that with her. She often told me that she was going to become a nurse so that she could heal herself. I sure wish that could have come true. Life for her and us started to change as we went through appointment after appointment, hospital stay after countless hospital stay. My heart continued to break in silence as I knew the time for her was ending. Then, one day while visiting her in the hospital, she had this big smile while telling our pastor and me that she saw "The Light" and wasn't afraid. I turned my internal sadness into joy because I knew she would go to a better place with no more pain. I started to spend even more time with her, bringing her favorite foods. Our last outing was going to the movie theater to see *Spider-Man*. This movie will forever be one of my favorites.

She ended up in the hospital and on a ventilator. I watched her take her last breath. I remember feeling sad and happy at the same time. She often told me about her final wishes by saying, "TeTe, just make me pretty." I did just that! Although she didn't need help in that department.

Although I feel empty most days without her after all these years, I have no regrets about letting her go. I made the most of the time we had left, and I wouldn't change it for the world. I realized something about myself during this time; I am stronger than I give myself credit for. I was responsible for her hair, make-up, and clothes as requested. It was her final wish.

The pain came when I faced the loss of my older and younger brothers to violence. Having someone taken from you sometimes is unbearable. I had to face the shock and undeniable truth that they were gone. Words cannot describe the pain and the emptiness I fight daily.

Would I feel different…

If I'd talk to them before they were killed.

If I'd seen them.

If I was able to love on them one last time.

I wish I had one last time. Some days I do a better job of managing my pain. But, other days are not good, especially when a song, smell, or holiday comes. A friend told me, and now I remind myself of these words, "It's okay, not being okay."

I now know very different types of pain and grief. Grief varies based on the relationship and the person's importance to you. The word of God says in Psalm 30:5, "Weeping may endure for a night but joy comes in the morning." I don't allow people to tell me when that joy will come. It may be in months, years, or days, but it will come—to you in your time, to me in mine. Grief isn't something you will get over; it is something you learn to live with daily, and each passing moment allows those days to get a little easier.

The death of my brothers, little sister, niece, and nephew almost took me out, but my mother's death paralyzed me. Staring at nothing as my own breath faded. Like with my niece, I had to watch this beautiful, outspoken, loving, caring, God-Fearing, hardworking, funny, wise, and energetic person wither to nothing.

I was with my mother when she took her last breath. However, a week before her transition, she told me she was going home when it was just her and me. I suspect she also saw the light, and she was ready to go be with her heavenly father. Although I wasn't prepared to hear this or ready for her to go, I told her that she was the best mother ever, she did a great job raising ten kids by herself, and I loved her so much. She too prepared me by letting me know her final wishes, and I was honored to attend to them.

I know she is free of pain and suffering, and I'm happy about that. I wish I could have just one more kiss on the forehead, one more hug, and one more talk, but I know "one more" would never be enough. I did the best I could when she needed me the most. I stay away from the "what-if" thoughts, so I can sleep at night. I do, however, wish I had someone who'd experienced the death of a mother warn me of the pain. But heck, I can't explain it! There are no words to describe this hurt. I wouldn't wish grief on my worst enemy.

Life goes on, but I wish it were all a dream and I could wake up from this nightmare one day. But I keep pushing through, remembering, and reflecting on the good times we shared and the thought that I will see her again.

At some point in life, grief touches everyone. If I'd lend any advice, it would be to keep moving. Live the way your loved one would want you to. Many days you might not be okay. But it is okay not to be okay. Joy comes in the morning. Find treasure in the memories and joy in the privilege of knowing them. My people are with me.

My mother.

My brothers.

My sister.

My niece.

My nephew.

Because I carry them in my heart.

Impacted

As told by Megan Erskine

Brilliant and complicated would be the words used to describe my mother. She was a great educator. She had many challenges growing up, but her resilience made her the woman I am so proud to call my mom. I know my drive to champion the underdog came from her. When I reflect on all the great things she did in her lifetime, I wonder if she knew the impact she made.

My mother was the youngest child of Dutch immigrants that arrived in America in 1954. She was one of five kids and the only child born in the United States. Education was a top priority, and there was a lot of pressure on her to achieve. Because she was the only "American" in the family, her parents expected more from her. Her childhood was hard because she was significantly younger than her older siblings, and she cared for her parents early. She did not speak English until she entered kindergarten. The family had limited resources, and they often struggled for money. Her parents survived the horror of WWII in Amsterdam, and that trauma, unfortunately, impacted their family dynamic.

My mom went to college at the University of Illinois. She was very good at science and became a teacher. Throughout most of her teaching career, she taught in rural communities. She was an incredible teacher. She won a lot of awards. She had a gift for helping people understand things. People truly loved her, and she loved people. A bizarre thing happened to me when I worked at Columbia College in 2008, years after her death. I was having a bad day. I was in the photography building and got off the elevator on the wrong floor. When I went into the stairwell to get to the right floor, there were these giant black-and-white pictures of my mom. A photography professor purchased a vintage yearbook at a garage sale and had the pictures blown up and printed to advertise the digital lab. The pictures were beautiful. You could see in the pictures how much she enjoyed her students, and they enjoyed her. She truly loved what she did. When I told my dad about it, he said the yearbook was from a school that no longer existed. It was my mom's first teaching job.

I read somewhere that people with childhood trauma become the adults they wish they had around when they were kids. I think that is why my mom was such a good teacher. She went above and beyond teaching and gave a lot of lost kids a safe place to land. When she was teaching in rural Pennsylvania, she had students that were living in their cars. She would cook breakfast for them before school. The principal of the school was upset about it. My mom didn't waver. My mom kept feeding those kids. To others, they were throw-away kids, but to her, they just needed a little help. She was always willing to help. We lived in an area where domestic violence was a huge problem. My mother started a shelter for battered women. She rescued animals all the time. If there was a need and she could help, she did. I remember that one of her old students gave her a wall hanging with a hobo symbol of a cat, which means that "a kind lady lives here." The cat symbol alerted hobo travelers to where they could find help or support.

My sisters and I were all born in Pennsylvania. My mom had supported my dad through veterinary school and his PhD program. When we moved to Alabama, she decided to get her master's degree in botany. We only stayed there two years. We then moved to Michigan. I think she started to feel resentful that she put my dad through school when she was just as capable of getting an advanced degree. I also think she had something to prove to her father. So she decided to return to school to earn her PhD, and she moved us back to Alabama without my father. Those were the worst and best days of my life. She worked, went to school, and raised three daughters. We went to school in Alabama and lived with our dad in

Michigan during the summers. She was an amazing woman who could handle it all. I also remember this was as a time when my mom's mental health challenges became apparent to me.

I remember knowing at 12 that my mom would die young. As the oldest, I had to parent her a lot. In Alabama, there were days that she felt really depressed and wouldn't leave her room. We would clean up because we thought she was sad because the house was dirty. Eventually, we moved back to Michigan because my parents thought it was better for them to be together. I'm not sure if it was better for her.

My freshman year of high school, I tried to rebel… sort of. I skipped a class, bringing my grade to an A-. She was emotionally distraught. A lot of the pressure she felt as a child to achieve was coming out in her own parenting. I remember her saying my life was ruined. From then on, I worked hard to ensure I was a straight A student. I played every varsity sport and joined clubs. My mom designed my identity, and I skipped the normal teen rebellion phase that allows people to carve out who they are. Although she was the most loving parent, our codependency made adolescence challenging.

In my senior year, I came home one day, and my mom was sitting on the sofa crying with my uncle Tim. My uncle Tim was her favorite sibling. I remember her saying, "I'm sorry, I'm sorry." My mother had been diagnosed with stage 4 colon cancer. She was dying, and there was nothing that could be done. We were all thrown for a loop. We were about to lose the parent who poured her whole life into us.

My uncle Tim died very suddenly two weeks before my mom. She died on February 27, 2003, while I was in college. I was very lost and made many bad decisions in my grief. I self-harmed a lot. Of course, I missed her a lot, but because so much of my life had been directed by her, I struggled with identity and decision-making.

Processing my mother's death has been challenging for my family. We've experienced every emotion that grief offers between the four of us. My relationship with my sisters is very strong, and I don't think we would be as close if our mom was still around. We've all healed in our own ways, and I think we're better people for it. We miss our mom a lot. We were her world. I think our grief made us who we are today. I struggle when I am proud of who my sisters and I have become, knowing that our mother's death helped shape us. I feel bad knowing that we are thriving now, and she doesn't get to enjoy us as full-grown people. Especially since she did most of the early childhood parenting. I know she would be proud of us, and I am thankful she was my mother. She made a huge impact on the world in a short amount of time.

My Heart

Eleanor Brown

I SHOULDN'T HAVE LEFT.

Those words will always ring loud when I remember the day my mother died. Our house phone rang late at night, and my father answered. He was understandably upset. His wife, our mother, our Queen, My Heart, was gone. My father gathered himself and headed to the hospital. Her soul wasn't there, but we had to see about her body. My memories following my mother's death don't consist of much of her services. My 16-year-old mind could only focus on My Heart being gone.

How could this be happening? I know how. But how?

I needed her.

There was so much life for me to live. I was only a junior in high school. Within the next year, I'd be preparing for what was supposed to be the most exciting events of my high school years. Prom and graduation.

For many teenagers, prom is a big deal. For girls, it's the wedding before the wedding. You decide on the perfect dress and shoes. You get dolled up by getting your hair, nails, and make-up done. People come to see you off. It's an exciting time. Not for me. I participated but with no joy. How could I find joy in anything My Heart couldn't participate in.

You should be here.

I wanted my mom here every step of the way. Whether her input was requested or not, I wanted to hear it. I wanted to hear my mom say, "You look beautiful." Help me put my dress on and zip me up. Present me to the world like a princess. It didn't happen then or at my wedding years later. My mom missed more life milestones than she was alive to witness. High school graduation is one of them.

"Did she know?"

She raised us to live without her. Maybe her strong connection with God made her know that her "forever" wouldn't be on Earth. She didn't waste time entertaining things that didn't matter. She was committed to teaching us the life lessons that could be corrupted if we learned them from anywhere else. Her open communication was never watered down. She gave it to us raw and uncut. It's appreciated now.

There was no escaping it, as both my parents were in ministry. Mama had a strong gift of prayer, intercession, and spiritual deliverance. Prayer was often the background noise at our house. When working with someone, she would call us into the room to see and understand what could happen if we got too far from God. This developed sensitivity in me to spiritual matters. We were to stay close to God and always depend on him.

As I grew older, that foundation was lifesaving. No one would believe it because I fell into depression. I can't pinpoint when it started. I was sad when my mom died, but my sadness turned into anger somewhere along the line. Today I can be honest about my anger toward God. Everything I'd been taught growing up told me it was wrong. But I felt how I felt. I didn't talk about it. Who was there to listen? Who? I isolated myself and turned into a workaholic. By that time, I was in my twenties and had the perfect mask. My own joy wasn't present, and I hid behind the joy I could give other women by doing their hair.

I recognized my talent, but my purpose was lost in darkness. This unsafe place was not for me. Mama warned me. I had to detour before I ended up like the people she helped. God's grace kept me, even when I didn't want to be kept. I am thankful. Prayer and meditation became my lifeline. I'd get lost in the presence of God through worship. The more I communed with God, the more my darkness faded away. I began to find balance because I was no longer avoiding my grief. My healing was no longer held hostage.

When I started healing, I could incorporate things that reminded me of my mom into my life. I'd purchase her favorite perfume so I could smell her scent. Some days I wore the perfume. Growing up, I spent a lot of time in the kitchen cooking with her. Now, I cook some of her signature dishes. It makes me feel close to her. It's also an opportunity to get family together. We all miss her. We take the chance any time we have it to just be together and love one another the way she would if she was here. We share stories. Since I am younger, my siblings have more memories. I enjoy listening to them paint a mural of all the love my mom poured into each one. I just listen and smile.

I've come a long way since the night of that phone call. I miss my mother more than anything in the world. There is so much I wish I could tell her. Things I wish she could advise me on, but she left me in good hands. I have godmothers and aunts that have done a great job of being mother figures. They never tried to be my mom. They ensured I had options when I felt like I needed a maternal presence. God, on the other hand, isn't an option. He is a necessity. Psalm 18:2 says, "The Lord is my rock, my fortress, and my deliverer; my God, my strength, in whom I will trust; my buckler, and the horn of my salvation, and my high tower." God had been everything I didn't know I needed all my life. There is no way I would be who I am without him, grief and all.

Thirty Percent

As told by Pastor Monté Dillard

We must learn how to grieve. There are things to stay away from and margins that we all should remain between. The goal is never to diminish anyone's grief, but with it being unending, there are some roads that we don't want to go down. Sorrow can happen regularly, so finding a healthy way to manage it is imperative. As a pastor, you aren't just helping people through grief; you are often grieving yourself. Our church experienced the loss of a member on January 1, 2022. It was not news expected to hear just a few hours after preaching for our New Year's Eve service. I don't have enough fingers for the number of funerals or memorials we've been at since then. It comes with the responsibility of pastoring a large church. When I lose a member of my church, I help their family while feeling it myself. That results in sharpening the skill of proper grief management. With it happening so often, I must remain physically and emotionally available when called to help.

Another significant component of it is the theology surrounding death. It often provokes questions. As their pastor, I may not have the answers to many of those questions. I must be okay with that. People are baffled by God's activity or lack of activity in someone's death. People may feel like God took the person, or God could have preserved, healed, or kept them from dying. We try to find ways to enlighten them. Encouraging people with Philippians 4:13, "You can do all things through Christ Jesus." It doesn't mean you won't hurt or have tough times. You absolutely will. Make up your mind that God had not put this on you while not giving you the strength to carry it. People also should find sustainable ways to process their grief. Whether that is through therapy or a clergy person that can walk with them through a season of processing. Sometimes neither option is accepted. The prayer then becomes, Lord, keep them until they are ready.

I have worked to be more learned in not just what the Bible says, but what scriptures mean. The Bible instructs us to stand firm, but there is no expectation that we do not grieve and be affected by the loss. In John 11, we see a sequence of events supporting that.

Jesus allows Lazarus to die.

Tells His disciples, I'm going to wake him up. Meaning raising him from the dead.

He gets to Lazarus's tomb and cries; Jesus wept.

Jesus felt the pain of his friend dying.

Another scripture related to grief is "Blessed are those who mourn." No scripture says blessed are those who don't mourn. The scripture acknowledges mourning. We must have healthy theology of grief. Reminding people that to feel grief is not a dereliction of faith. Crying doesn't mean you don't trust God. Trust increases as He keeps you through your loss. We must be clear about what grief is and isn't. Grief is the pain experienced at losing something or someone significant and deeply loved in their life. We will all lose something or someone. Grief isn't just only about losing people. In pastoral ministry, you help people grieve many things in many ways. I've counseled people who've been divorced. There is grief that comes with that type of loss. I've heard that divorce is like someone dying, but you will keep seeing them. If someone works at a company for 30 or 40 years and retires, grief may be associated with that transition. People struggle with losing something that has been a big part of their life, most of their life. Geographical moves come with a certain level of grief. A child goes off to college after living at home all their life. Losing people is the most common way I help people grieve, but people suffer many things. I help people manage those emotions.

Thirty percent of my pastoral work during the week can be centered around grief. Much of this loss I am deeply impacted by. I have relationships with these people. To remain effective in my pastoral role, I am careful of how far I go into grief. I can't pastorally carry everyone's suffering and be emotionally available when the next family needs me. Taking on everyone's grief is not humanly possible without killing you. Not to imply that I don't feel any of it. Over the years, we've lost many members of our church. I must be intentional about how I balance my own grief. There are times when the scale can tilt.

A member of our church lost his mother some years ago. He was a pretty "tough" guy. I watched him as the lid of the casket was closed. I will never forget the look on his face. As he walked toward her coffin, I thought he would stop the funeral directors. At that moment, I wanted to cry with him. I remember feeling the Holy Spirit yank me back, reminding me I had work to do. That man was hurt, and there was something in me that wanted to let him know; I feel it with you. Yet the Holy Spirit wouldn't allow me to. If I had lived in that moment with him, I would have lost ground for what I needed to do and lead him. It's not always easy. There have been plenty of times I've been unable to keep it together.

My primary way to process the things in my heart, including but not limited to something I'm grieving, is in devotion. It is my time to lay things down. This helps me determine what settles in my heart. Pastors grieve the ability to grieve. To do this work, you have to be okay that you'll never really get to grieve as many people as you probably would like. There is a level of detachment necessary to keep going. Denying ourselves the ability to feel some things to remain effective. Pastors don't get the privilege to fully feel the loss of everyone we know and love. Nobody tells you this when going into pastoring. All you are taught is how to write and deliver a sermon.

The call to ministry comes with the grace to do it. Pastoral ministry can kill you. Not figuratively. Not hyperbole.

You will die.

There is emotional intelligence you must have.

Emotional boundaries you must have.

    The psychological component.

       The physical toll on your body

         You must constantly be forgiving.

           All while being genuine…

             Reminding yourself of why you do it

I learned balance from the Holy Spirit. John 14:26 tells us that the Advocate will teach us everything and remind us of God's words. The Holy Spirit taught me how to create levels of emotional detachment. I talk to the Lord about every aspect of my life because He knows everything. The Holy Spirit will help shift your perspective. We can approach life with the mindset of "God, why do I have to go through this." We also have the option to have the attitude of "God, thank you for being with me as I go through this." This is the counsel I use with people whenever they are experiencing any life challenge. I'm grateful that I don't have to do this work alone. I am confident that this perspective will help others as well.

Acknowledgments

God, you did it. Thank you for trusting me with this assignment.

When God planted the seed for this project, I didn't share it with anyone. I needed to see this baby birthed, and I was afraid to tell the wrong person and it wouldn't come to pass. I felt lead to share with Enyd Scott. I told Enyd about the project but explained that I had no idea how to start. A few weeks later, Enyd called me and said, "So you know your project, let's do it." She has shared in every moment and pushed me when I lost momentum or felt discouraged. Enyd taught me that a win is a win, no matter how small. She also taught me that lessons are wins.
Enyd, this book is as much yours as it is mine.
Thank you!

Thank you, Elect Lady Tina Dillard, for being the spiritual covering over this project. I knew that I needed someone praying for and with me. You are appreciated.

Thank you to the focus group members that volunteered their time to read and discuss each entry, Debbie Allen, Aimee Gonzalez, Glenford Gordon, Tamara Hadaway.

To my village! Thank you!

Each person that contributed to this book is celebrated. Your vulnerability and willingness to share a dark moment of your life is nothing to be taken lightly. My ongoing prayer is that each of you continue to heal from the trauma of grief.

Contributors

Debbie Allen is first and foremost a Child of God! She is the mother and grandmother of the most wonderful people God ever blew breath into. She loves art, books, creativity, and laughter! She is grateful for being able to use all the crayons in her box to create the picture that is her life.

Alea Allen is a native of Evanston, Illinois. A dedicated Educator for over 20 years, Alea is passionate about making a difference in the lives of the youth who will become the leaders of tomorrow. "There's a purpose for my pain that is connected to God's Promise for my life and those connected to me."

Shaun Carr is a lifelong resident of Chicago, Illinois. Although born and raised on Chicago's West Side, he has resided on the city's South Side since 2001. In his spare time, he enjoys video gaming, classical & jazz music, following political news on cable television & talk radio, and being a loving pet parent to his 2 kittens.

Laurie Carrier has dedicated her medical career to caring for disproportionally affected communities. Her passion project is figuring out ways to combat burnout and make this challenging work easier for all. When not working, she loved spending time with her family, either in Chicago or exploring the world through travel.

Andrea Corley-Gardner is a proud wife, mother of three, and grandmother. In her free time, she enjoys entertaining friends and family, watching action and comedy movies. She also enjoys praise dancing for the Lord.

Eleanor Crawford Brown is from the south side of Chicago, Illinois. Her love for making women look good and feel good

143

about themselves has led her to a 23-year career as a licensed hairstylist. She has been owner/proprietor of "I'm Finally Please Beauty Salon" for 12 years. Eleanor loves to sing and lead people into a worship experience with the Lord.

Tracy Cruz is the beloved wife of her late husband, William Cruz. She lives in Georgia with her baby dogs Mitzi and Jack. She was blessed with a marriage from God, who designed it how it is supposed to be, one flesh. She really lived that out with "My William" God's love.

Pastor Monté Dillard serves as the Senior Pastor of First Church of God Christian Life Center. Pastoring God's people remains a passion and top priority. He also is a skilled speaker, consultant, chaplain, and provides spiritual guidance in personal, marital, and pre-marital counseling. Believing that the church is only as strong as the family, his primary focus is his family. He and his wife Tina are blessed with four children. www.montedillard.com

Tina Dillard resides in Evanston Illinois, but was born and raised in East Chicago, Indiana. She's the wife of Pastor Monté L.G. Dillard of First Church of God Christian Life Center. A stay home mom of 18 years, to her four beautiful children. Nia, Kennedi, Morgan, & Monté Jr. In her spare time, she enjoys cooking and teaching step aerobics classes at her local YMCA.

Jamie Ellingwood lives in Chicago with her furry sidekick, Jojo. She enjoys volunteering at a local greenhouse, tending to her own vegetable garden, traveling, hiking, and exploring new foods and places.

Megan Erskine is a daughter and a sister who loves a cozy day, driving in a foreign country, and rescuing dogs off the side of the road. She loves a good story and a laugh.

Ikari Gardner Sr. is a husband, father of three sons, and grandfather to one. He is a minister of the Gospel of Jesus

Christ and an employee of a utility company in the Chicagoland area for 22 years. He enjoys cooking barbeque and vacationing with his family.

Rachel Porter is a wife, mother, entrepreneur, and psalmist. Native of Chicago Illinois, Rachel strives to be present and vibrantly focused on her entrepreneurial task! Founder and creator of ScRaWny RaGs LLC and Cover Me' Baby® is her most current endeavor. She gives all Praise to God!

DeAnna Gibson is a wife, dog mom, daughter, sister, friend, entrepreneur, and Minister of the Gospel of Jesus. Born and raised in the Midwest. She enjoys working out, taking trips, and making people feel good about themselves.

Katie Greer is a fervent grief coach, educator, and founder of Satellight Project LLC. She champions loss survivors through their unique experiences. She serves on an Educational Foundation, local PTA, and Trauma Intervention Program NW. Katie delights in hobby farming, kitchen dancing, and front porch conversations blended with coffee and laughter.

Yolanda Harris is a wife, mother, and grandmother. She has a passion for the healing and liberty of battered women and has always been willing to serve in recovery for that great cause.

Nicole Henry is a loving mom and entrepreneur who lives in Evanston, Illinois. In her free time, she enjoys poetry, listening to podcasts, and mommy and daughter dates.

Monique Jackson, is a single mom of one. Native New Yorker, a serial entrepreneur who loves the Lord and doesn't lean unto her understanding. Though she never saw it coming and grief never goes away, she's learned it Gets Easier!

Amber Johnson is a creative soul with a sweet spirit. She is the proud business owner of Amber Danielle Photography. In her free time, she loves to cook, watch movies, and listen to music. www.amberdaniellephotography.com

Cheryl Johnson is a minister of the Gospel of Jesus Christ and the proud mother of two entrepreneurial daughters, a Photographer, and a children's book writer. In her free time, Cheryl loves to watch old movies, create new recipes and work on 1000+ puzzles.

Karena Leonard is a mother of 3 adult children and 4 grandchildren. She's caring and ambitious and loves the Lord, family, and friends, and looks forward to all that life has to offer.

Aixa Lopez, a Chicago native that puts God and family first. In her free time, she enjoys watching reality TV, crime shows with her mom and cooking with her mom and sisters. She recently became a fur mom, again, and is enjoying every second.

Luke Lucas lives on the North side of Chicago, Illinois, where he was born and raised. Luke currently oversees the Illinois switchboards for a healthcare system. When he is not working, he is recapping and commenting on TV shows for a couple of websites. www.bukebucas.org

Marisa McPherson is a mother of 2 boys, Joshua and Jordan. In her free time, she enjoys dancing, cooking, and being with her boys.

Mellisa Michael is a proud mother of one son, Donté Jr. She believes in meeting people where they are and showing compassion and love. She is a Licensed Social Worker and is passionate about Maternal Mental Health and Woman Empowerment. In her free time, she likes to discover new recipes, indulge in self-care, and spend quality time with her son.

Eden Voigt is a college student living in Chicago. She enjoys drawing, listening to podcasts, and spending time with family, friends, and her cats Poppy and Logan in her free time. She aspires to become a teacher upon graduating.

Felicia Warner is a proud wife, sister, friend, mother of four beautiful daughters and six grandchildren, an entrepreneur, and a dedicated member of Mount Carmel Bible Church in Chicago, Illinois for over 40 years. A Chicago native, she is the CEO of Pure & Extreme Cleaning Services, LLC, and loves learning new things, volunteering, traveling, playing softball, running, and just living life to the fullest. Grief is never easy, but she always reminds herself that "It's Okay Not Being Okay."

E'a Williams is a proud mother of two boys but now a fresh empty nester further pursuing her artistic and wellness passion as a Social Entrepreneur through her movement called THUG Hippie, The Healing U Give. Teaching people how to heal using shared experiences to grow communities. E'a is a Performer, Yogi, Percussionist, Massage Therapist, Teaching Artist, healer!

Shaleka Smith was born and raised on the Northside of Chicago. Where she currently lives and is raising her daughter. She has worked in a healthcare setting for twelve years. Shaleka serves at her home church faithfully and is a preacher of the Gospel.

Shaleka believes that the key to life management is finding community. Though there are moments that we must endure alone, we need to have people around us that have empathy for the trauma and triumphs life brings. Community is imperative not just for bad times but more importantly for good times. Shaleka enjoys share good laughs with those around her. "If you ain't laughing, you ain't living."

Though "Grief, I Didn't Sign Up for This" is Shaleka's inaugural book, she is determined that there are many more.

Resources

Grief Share - https://www.griefshare.org/findagroup

> GriefShare is a friendly, caring group of people who will walk alongside you through one of life's most difficult experiences. You don't have to go through the grieving process alone.

National Suicide Prevention Lifeline – 1-800-273-8255

Crisis Text Line – Text HOME to 741-741

SAMHSA - https://www.samhsa.gov/find-help/national-helpline
(Substance Abuse and Mental Health Services Administration)

> SAMHSA's National Helpline is a free, confidential, 24/7, 365-day-a-year treatment referral and information service for individuals and families facing mental and/or substance use disorders. 1-800-662-HELP (4357)

Therapy for Back Girls - https://therapyforblackgirls.com

> Therapy for Black Girls is an online space dedicated to encouraging the mental wellness of Black women and girls.

Therapy for Black Men - https://therapyforblackmen.org

> At TherapyforBlackMen.org, we want to break the stigma that asking for help is a sign of weakness.